PLANT IDENTIFIERS

CLEMATIS & CLIMBERS

CLEMATIS & CLIMBERS

LANCE HATTATT

DP

DEMPSEY
PARR

This edition first published in 1999 by
Dempsey Parr
Queen Street House
4–5 Queen Street
Bath BA1 1HE

Conceived, edited, illustrated
and produced by Robert Ditchfield Publishers

ISBN 1 84084 337 3

A copy of the British Library Cataloguing in Publication
Data is available from the Library.

Typeset by Action Publishing Technology Ltd, Gloucester
Colour origination by Colour Quest Graphic Services Ltd,
London E9
Printed and bound in Hong Kong

Many of the plants were photographed in the author's garden:
The Arrow Cottage Garden
Near Weobley
Herefordshire HR4 8RN
Tel: 01544 318468

Half title page: *Clematis* 'Gravetye Beauty'
Frontispiece: *Clematis* 'Margot Koster'
Title page: *Rosa* 'Princesse Marie'
Contents page: *Crinodendron hookerianum*

CONTENTS

INTRODUCTION — 6

1. CLEMATIS — 14
   in alphabetical sequence

2. CLIMBERS — 114
   in alphabetical sequence

3. WALL PLANTS — 206
   in alphabetical sequence

INDEX OF COMMON NAMES — 255

INTRODUCTION

No GARDEN should be without a generous selection of clematis and climbers. Not only do they provide foliage and, most often, flower throughout the greater part of the year, but they add interest to numerous garden situations which would be denied with more conventional plantings of trees, shrubs or herbaceous perennials. This, of course, is on account of their versatility, the way in which they grow, for few other plants will climb or trail in the manner of these. Furthermore, at a time when gardens are, if anything, becoming smaller, they occupy very little space and so are, therefore, ideal for the times in which we live.

CHOOSING A CLIMBER

With so many climbers available from specialist nurseries or garden centres, making a choice as to what to include in the garden will always be a difficult decision. Much will depend on the situation in mind, whether the planting should be seasonal or more permanent, that is to say annual or perennial, deciduous or evergreen, for sun or shade, for flower or foliage. Additionally, colour will be a main consideration. It may be that the climber is to complement an existing planting scheme and will, because of this, fall within a particular colour range. On the other hand, none of this may matter, the dominant idea being to create something which totally exists in its own right. Yet again, it will not be possible to ignore the soil conditions which will,

Clematis, Abutilon and *Solanum* cover a wall in a white/lilac scheme.

whatever the case, dictate to a large degree what will grow where.

Allowing for all of these things, it will come as no surprise to find that the choice of what to include remains open and wide and that much pleasure will be gained from poring over garden books and catalogues, visiting gardens and nurseries, before the final selection is made.

SITUATION

It matters very little where climbers are sited providing

Clematis 'Gypsy Queen'

that their individual cultivation requirements are met. Walls, boundary hedges and fences, sheds, summerhouses, trellis, arch and pergola, all of these will immediately suggest themselves. So too will purpose-built pyramids, columns or obelisks. Perhaps less obvious is to use existing plants, particularly shrubs and trees, to act as hosts; to partner two very different climbers to support and grow through each other; or simply to peg climbers to the ground so that they trail through the borders horizontally rather than, as is more usual, climb vertically.

Whatever the situation, and it can be enormous fun to experiment with new, and possibly challenging, ideas, care should be taken to ensure that all climbers receive adequate water at all times according to their needs. So often when plants are placed against a wall, an overhanging roof can preclude rain from reaching the roots. Clematis, particularly, as well as enjoying a rich feed flourish most where the soil remains moist and is not allowed to dry out.

Some climbers will support themselves, often by means of leaf tendrils. Others will need to be tied in to supports. In these cases it often makes most sense to put some form of support framework in place before planting takes place. Where it is necessary to use ties, then these should be checked regularly to ensure that they are not cutting into stems.

LOOKING AFTER CLIMBERS

Once established, the majority of climbers will not be demanding in terms of attention. For many it will be enough to be given an annual feed and for commonsense, routine management to be undertaken. This will include the cutting out of any dead wood, the thinning of overcrowded branches and regular deadheading to promote, where appropriate, prolonged flowering.

Clematis do respond to specific treatment which is not, contrary to popular belief, at all difficult. Early flowering clematis require little pruning beyond the removal of weak and dead stems once flowering is over (in the following pages this procedure is given the symbol P1). Large flowered hybrids, blooming before midsummer, should be lightly pruned, which involves removing any tangled growth and generally thinning-out and tidying, after flowering (P2). Those flowering later, on the current season's stems, should be cut back hard to ground level over winter or in early spring. New, young shoots will shortly appear (P3). As a point of fact, all clematis should be planted deeply in humus-rich soil and should be kept well watered until established. Should a clematis suffer from wilt, the main symptom of which is the sudden collapse of an otherwise healthy plant, then cut to ground level, remove all diseased material, apply a sulphur-based fungicide, mulch heavily and water well. In the majority of cases the clematis will then throw up new shoots.

CLIMBERS FOR EFFECT

Planting schemes are without limit. Use all climbers in the garden to create new and imaginative effects, to enhance existing plantings as well as in the creation of new ones. Ignore preconceived ideas or out-of-date, hard and fast rules. Be bold and experiment. White flowers look startlingly brilliant against deep green; red, in the same situation, will be seductive. Purple, depending on its partner, may be regal, pensive or moody, whilst yellow will convey warmth and brilliance. Imagination and a sense of purpose, these are the only requirements to transform the garden, with the aid of climbers, into something exceptional and very beautiful.

OPPOSITE: A curtain of *Wisteria floribunda* hangs from an archway.

An early autumn picture of Virginia creeper weaving through ivy.

HOW TO USE THIS BOOK

Approximate measurements of a plant's height and spread are given in both metric and imperial measures. The height is the first measurement, as in for example 1.2m × 60cm/4 × 2ft. However, both height and spread vary so greatly from garden to garden since they depend on soil, climate, pruning and position (a plant grown in a container may well have its growth restricted), that these measurements are offered as guides only. This is especially true of trees and shrubs where ultimate growth can be unpredictable. Where only one measurement is given, this is height.

The following symbols are also used:

○	=	the plant thrives in or tolerates full sun.
◑	=	thrives in or tolerates part-shade.
●	=	thrives in or tolerates full shade.
◊	=	prefers well-drained soil.
◑	=	prefers moist soil (the text will state if the plant requires good drainage as well as moist soil, as is often the case).
●	=	prefers wet soil.
E	=	the plant is evergreen.
LH	=	needs acid soil and is intolerant of lime.
✳✳✳	=	the plant is fully hardy and can survive winters in temperate regions.
✳✳	=	the plant is only frost-hardy, not fully hardy and it is likely it will need shelter and protection during winter in temperate regions.
✳	=	the plant is tender (or half-hardy) and even in mild winter areas it may need protection to survive, or can be grown under glass.

POISONOUS PLANTS

In recent years, concern has been voiced about poisonous plants or plants which can cause allergic reactions if touched. The fact is that many plants are poisonous, some in a particular part, others in all their parts. For the sake of safety, it is always, without exception, essential to assume that no part of a plant should be eaten unless it is known, without any doubt whatsoever, that the plant or its part is edible and that it cannot provoke an allergic reaction in the individual person who samples it. It must also be remembered that some plants can cause severe dermatitis, blistering or an allergic reaction if touched, in some individuals and not in others. It is the responsibility of the individual to take all the above into account.

1.
CLEMATIS

Clematis 'Abundance'

A late flowering clematis producing striking mauve-pink flowers veined red on the current season's growth in mid and late summer. Use all of the late clematis to add colour and interest to borders at the approach of autumn.

Height × spread: Climbing or trailing to 3–3.5/10–12ft.

Soil: For any well drained but moist soil.

Position: Suitable for planting against a wall, to climb into a shrub or tree or to trail through the border where it will associate happily with late flowering perennials.

Care: Hard prune to ground level in early spring. Enrich annually with garden compost or well rotted manure. Keep well watered in dry periods.

| ○ ◑ | ◊ | ❄❄❄ | P3 |

Clematis 'Alba Luxurians'

A late flowering clematis producing eye-catching flowers of pure white, tipped with green, and with a pronounced eye of purple stamens in mid and late summer. Use to great effect in a border predominantly of white and green. Most attractive when partnered with *Hydrangea arborescens* 'Annabelle'.

Height × spread: Climbing or trailing to 3–3.5m/10–12ft.

Soil: For any well drained but moist soil.

Position: Suitable for planting against a wall, to climb into a shrub or tree or to trail through the border.

Care: Hard prune to ground level in early spring. Enrich annually with garden compost or well rotted manure. Keep well watered in dry periods.

◯ ◐ | ◗ | ❄❄❄ | P3

Clematis alpina

An easy, early flowering clematis producing deep purple-blue nodding bell-type flowers in spring, later to be followed by fluffy seedheads. This species clematis is a welcome addition to any spring border.

Height × spread: Climbing or trailing to 2–2.4m/6–8ft.

Soil: For any well drained but moist soil.

Position: Will thrive in a shady or cool spot where it is well suited to climbing into a shrub or tree or to trail through the border. Useful for a position receiving little if any sun.

Care: Remove unwanted growth after flowering and before midsummer. Enrich annually with garden compost or well rotted manure. Keep well watered in dry periods.

◐ ● | ◊ | ❀❀❀ | P1

An early flowering clematis producing semi-double
flowers of mid-blue, slightly larger than the species, in
spring. Suitable for pot cultivation where it will serve to
add height and act as a focus if given some support.
Surround it in a pot with complementary or contrasting
winter pansies.

Height × spread: Climbing or trailing to 2–2.4m/6–8ft.

Soil: For any well drained but moist soil.

Position: Suitable for planting against a wall, to climb into a shrub or
tree or to trail through the border.

Care: Remove unwanted growth after flowering and before
midsummer. Enrich annually with garden compost or well rotted manure.
Keep well watered in dry periods.

◯◑ ⬤ ❄❄❄ P1

Clematis alpina 'Ruby'

An early, vigorous, spring flowering clematis with small
lantern flowers of dusky rose with cream anthers. An ideal
clematis to allow the freedom of a spring border where it
will be happy to twine amongst early perennials and
bulbs.

Height × spread: Climbing or trailing to 3m/10ft.

Soil: For any well drained but moist soil.

Position: Will tolerate shade, where the flower colour is inclined to
be less intense. Otherwise suitable for planting against a wall, to climb
into a shrub or tree or to trail through the border.

Care: Remove unwanted growth after flowering and before
midsummer. Enrich annually with garden compost or well rotted manure.
Keep well watered in dry periods.

◐◑ ◖ ❋❋❋ P1

Clematis alpina 'Willy'

An early, vigorous, spring flowering clematis. Nodding flowers are of pale mauve-pink with distinctive cerise-pink markings to each sepal. Unusual colourings, such as are to be found here, serve to lift a border and to provide added interest.

Height × spread: Climbing or trailing to 2–2.4m/6–8ft.

Soil: For any well drained but moist soil.

Position: Suitable for planting against a wall, to climb into a shrub or tree or to trail through the border where it may readily be controlled with judicious pruning each year.

Care: Remove unwanted growth after flowering and before midsummer. Enrich annually with garden compost or well rotted manure. Keep well watered in dry periods.

Clematis 'Arabella'

A late flowering clematis producing open flowers of violet-mauve, later fading to violet-blue, with a distinctive eye of cream stamens in mid and late summer. A most pleasing effect is achieved when this clematis is partnered with pale lemon, such as the flowers of *Santolina chamaecyparissus* 'Lemon Queen'.

Height × **spread:** Climbing or trailing to 2–2.4m/6–8ft.

Soil: For any well drained but moist soil.

Position: Suitable for planting against a wall, to climb into a shrub or tree or to trail through the border where it will associate happily with late flowering perennials.

Care: Hard prune to ground level in early spring. Enrich annually with garden compost or well rotted manure. Keep well watered in dry periods.

○ ◑ | ◊ | ✳✳✳ | P3

Clematis 'Arctic Queen'

An appealing clematis producing lovely double, creamy-white flowers in early summer. Well suited to pot cultivation if given suitable support as shown here where it is positioned against a small, purpose-built obelisk.

Height × spread: Climbing or trailing to 2–2.4m/6–8ft.

Soil: For any well drained but moist soil.

Position: Grow against a pergola, trellis, or similar, or allow to climb into a shrub or tree where, flowering among lower branches, it will prolong the period of interest.

Care: Light prune in early spring when any dead wood should be removed. Enrich annually with garden compost or well rotted manure. Keep well watered in dry periods.

◐ ◑ | ◊ | ✳✳✳ | P2

Clematis armandii

An evergreen clematis of vigorous habit with handsome, leathery foliage and valued especially for its strongly scented white flowers in early spring. Not always easy to establish, plant deeply in humus-rich compost.

Height × spread: Climbing with some support to 4.5m/15ft.

Soil: For any well drained but moist soil.

Position: Plant in a sheltered spot in full sun out of the reach of cold winds which have a tendency to brown leaves. Cut these out immediately. Unsuitable for exposed areas.

Care: Remove unwanted growth and any weak or dead stems after flowering. Enrich annually with garden compost or well rotted manure. Keep well watered in dry periods.

◖ ◉ E ❄❄❄ P1

An unusual and seldom seen semi-herbaceous clematis of moderate growth. Violet-blue flowers, touched with deep red, appear in mid and late summer and carry a slight lemon scent.

Height × spread: Trailing with some support to 1–1.5m/3–5ft.

Soil: For any well drained but moist soil.

Position: Suitable for a mixed border in a sunny position. Use pea sticks to provide some necessary support or intermix with other plantings.

Care: Hard prune to ground level in early spring. Enrich annually with garden compost or well rotted manure. Keep well watered in dry periods. Apply a thick mulch in winter in cold areas for added protection.

| ◯ | ◌ | ❄❄❄ (borderline) | P3 |

An unusual hybrid clematis which deserves to be better known and more widely grown. Flowering freely in late spring and early summer, with repeat flowers in late summer into autumn, the large blooms are rose-pink at the outer edges lightening to blush at the centre and marked with a white bar.

Height × spread: Climbing or trailing to 2–2.4m/6–8ft.

Soil: For any well drained but moist soil.

Position: Suitable for planting against a wall, to climb into a shrub or tree or to trail through the border.

Care: Remove unwanted growth after flowering and before midsummer. Enrich annually with garden compost or well rotted manure. Keep well watered in dry periods.

○ ◑ | ◐ | ❅❅❅ | P1

Clematis 'Barbara Dibley'

Deep purple buds open to an unusual purple-magenta flower with darker tints on this spring and early summer flowering clematis. Of moderate growth, it generally fails to develop in bushiness. Use other plantings to conceal stems.

Height × spread: Climbing or trailing to 2m/6ft.

Soil: For any well drained but moist soil.

Position: Suitable for planting against a wall or to climb into a shrub or the lower branches of a tree or to trail through the border. Best in partial shade to prevent the flowers fading to a dull magenta-blue in full sunlight.

Care: Light prune in early spring when any dead wood should be removed. Enrich annually with garden compost or well rotted manure. Keep well watered in dry periods.

◑ ◐ ❄❄❄ P2

Clematis 'Barbara Jackman'

A vigorous, early summer flowering clematis with large flowers of mauve-blue with a deep, unpronounced magenta bar and an eye of cream stamens. Forms a bushy plant of good shape. Flowers intermittently again in autumn.

Height × spread: Climbing or trailing to 2.4m/8ft.

Soil: For any well drained but moist soil.

Position: Suitable for planting against a wall or to climb into a shrub or the lower branches of a tree or to trail through the border.

Care: Light prune in early spring when any dead wood should be removed. Enrich annually with garden compost or well rotted manure. Keep well watered in dry periods.

◐ ◐ | ⬥ | ❄❄❄ | P2

Flowers of this hybrid clematis are of an intense violet-blue, touching on purple, and are, in the early summer, double. Later, in late summer and early autumn, flowers are single, as shown here. Growth, unlike flowering, tends to be restricted.

Height × spread: Climbing or trailing to 1.5–2m/5–6ft.

Soil: For any well drained but moist soil.

Position: Suitable for planting against a wall or to climb into a shrub or the lower branches of a tree.

Care: Light prune in early spring when any dead wood should be removed. Enrich annually with garden compost or well rotted manure. Keep well watered in dry periods.

◐ ◑ | ◊ | ❄❄❄ | P2

Clematis 'Blue Bird'

Fresh green leaves complement the appealing, clear blue, nodding flowers of this early spring flowering clematis. An ideal climber to grow into a shrub or to scramble into an evergreen tree where it will add a further dimension.

Height × spread: Climbing or trailing to 2–2.4m/6–8ft.

Soil: For any well drained but moist soil.

Position: Suitable for planting against a wall, to climb into a shrub or tree or to trail through the border. May also be grown in the rock garden. Not unhappy in partial shade.

Care: Remove unwanted growth after flowering and before midsummer. Enrich annually with garden compost or well rotted manure. Keep well watered in dry periods.

◯◐ ◊ ❄❄❄ P1

Not dissimilar to *C. viticella* of which it is a close relation, this vigorous clematis produces bell-like flowers of white tinged with violet over attractive, fresh green foliage. On juvenile plants the flowers may appear completely white; this is a temporary stage of the plant's development.

Height × spread: Climbing or trailing to 4.5m/15ft.

Soil: For any well drained but moist soil.

Position: Suitable for planting against a wall or to climb into a shrub or tree.

Care: Hard prune to ground level in early spring. Enrich annually with garden compost or well rotted manure. Keep well watered in dry periods.

◯◑ ◊ ✳✳✳ P3

Clematis chrysocoma

An early summer flowering clematis closely resembling a *C. montana* in appearance but of less vigour. Pale pink flowers, somewhat deeper towards the centre, are carried over attractive foliage, the young leaves of which are noticeably bronze. A small, second flush of flowers follows in late summer.

Height × **spread:** Climbing or trailing to 6m/20ft.

Soil: For any well drained but moist soil.

Position: Suitable for planting against a wall or to climb into a shrub or tree.

Care: Remove unwanted growth after flowering and before midsummer. Enrich annually with garden compost or well rotted manure. Keep well watered in dry periods.

○ ◑ | ◖ | ❋❋❋ | P1

Clematis cirrhosa

One of the earliest of clematis producing hanging, nodding flowers of green-white fully opening to light cream in late winter and early spring. Evergreen leaves are small and slightly glossy in appearance but may be killed during periods of extreme cold.

Height × spread: Climbing or trailing to 4.5m/15ft.

Soil: For any well drained but moist soil.

Position: In colder areas afford the protection of a wall, against which it may be planted, in full sun. In mild, warm areas it will tolerate a shady aspect.

Care: Remove unwanted growth after flowering and before midsummer. Enrich annually with garden compost or well rotted manure. Keep well watered in dry periods.

| ○ ◑ | ◐ | E | ❋❋❋ (borderline) | P1 |

Clematis 'Comtesse de Bouchaud'

The popularity of this distinctive clematis is constant.
Easy to grow, it produces a mass of slightly textured,
ribbed, deep pink flowers in mid and late summer.
Although growing strongly it is, in fact, of limited height
so should be supported by something in scale with its
size.

Height × spread: Climbing or trailing to 2–2.4m/6–8ft.

Soil: For any well drained but moist soil.

Position: Suitable for planting against a wall or to climb into a shrub
or tree.

Care: Hard prune to ground level in early spring. Enrich annually with
garden compost or well rotted manure. Keep well watered in dry
periods.

| ◯ ◑ | ◊ | ❋ ❋ ❋ | P3 |

Clematis crispa

A slight clematis but one which is seldom seen and which deserves to be more widely grown. Flowers, appearing from early summer until autumn although in no great number, are slightly nodding and consist of four, lightly ribbed sepals, strongly reflexed, in shades of lilac-blue.

Height × spread: Climbing or trailing to 2–2.4m/6–8ft.

Soil: For any well drained but moist soil.

Position: Best suited to growing through a small shrub in a warm, sheltered situation.

Care: Hard prune to ground level in early spring. Enrich annually with garden compost or well rotted manure. Keep well watered in dry periods. Apply a thick mulch in winter in cold areas for added protection.

◐ ◖ ❄❄❄ (borderline) P3

Clematis 'Dr. Ruppel'

Exceedingly large flowers of rose-pink, overlaid with carmine, are the mark of this early clematis which reliably flowers for a second time in the autumn. Strong in growth and free flowering, 'Dr. Ruppel' may be relied upon to produce an eye-catching display.

Height × spread: Climbing or trailing to 2–3m/6–10ft.

Soil: For any well drained but moist soil.

Position: Suitable for planting against a wall, to cover a pergola, trellis, or similar, or to climb into a shrub or tree.

Care: Light prune in early spring when any dead wood should be removed. Enrich annually with garden compost or well rotted manure. Keep well watered in dry periods.

◯ ◑ | ◊ | ✿✿✿ | P2

Clematis 'Duchess of Albany'

Flowering from late summer through into autumn, this attractive clematis carries outward facing, bell-shaped flowers of mid-pink overlaid with rose-pink bars. Leaves are noticeably grey-green.

Height × spread: Climbing or trailing to 2–2.4m/6–8ft.

Soil: For any well drained but moist soil.

Position: Suitable for planting against a wall but particularly effective when allowed to scramble through a shrub or to trail through the border where, on account of its habit, it is easily managed.

Care: Hard prune to ground level in early spring. Enrich annually with garden compost or well rotted manure. Keep well watered in dry periods.

○ ◑ | ◐ | ❋❋❋ | P3

Clematis 'Duchess of Edinburgh'

An early summer flowering clematis with spectacular, fully double white flowers, the tiered sepals surrounding an eye of stamens of deep cream. Unfortunately, 'Duchess of Edinburgh' is often slow to establish and is, in comparison with many other clematis, short lived.

Height × spread: Climbing or trailing to 1.5–2m/5–6ft.

Soil: For any well drained but moist soil.

Position: Suitable for planting against a wall or to climb into a shrub or tree.

Care: Light prune in early spring when any dead wood should be removed. Enrich annually with garden compost or well rotted manure. Keep well watered in dry periods.

◔ ◑ | ◔ | ✳✳✳ | P2

Although it will flower on old wood, this clematis is best hard pruned for a fine display of carmine-red blooms on the current season's growth in midsummer. Stamens of bright cream contrast with the red of the sepals.

Height × spread: Climbing or trailing to 3.5m/12ft.

Soil: For any well drained but moist soil.

Position: Suitable for planting against a wall, to cover a pergola, trellis, or similar, or to climb into a shrub or tree.

Care: Hard prune to ground level in early spring. Enrich annually with garden compost or well rotted manure. Keep well watered in dry periods.

From midsummer through to autumn, this clematis carries a mass of deep violet-indigo flowers with furled yellow stamens over darkly green, tapering leaves. It is somewhat difficult to manage as its stems are non-clinging, apt to become tangled and are easily damaged by wind.

Height × **spread:** Climbing or trailing to 1–1.2m/3–4ft.

Soil: For any well drained but moist soil.

Position: Suitable for scrambling through the lower branches of a shrub or to trail through the border among herbaceous perennials.

Care: Hard prune to ground level in early spring. Enrich annually with garden compost or well rotted manure. Keep well watered in dry periods.

| ○ ◐ | ◐ | ✻✻✻ | P3 |

Clematis 'Elsa Späth'

Noted for its free flowering habit, this easy clematis produces a mass of deep lavender-blue flowers, gradually fading to a lighter shade, in profusion in midsummer and again reasonably in autumn. Grow 'Elsa Späth' for dramatic impact.

Height × spread: Climbing or trailing to 2–2.4m/6–8ft.

Soil: For any well drained but moist soil.

Position: Suitable for planting against a wall or to climb into a shrub or tree. May also be sited to cover an obelisk or other free-standing structure.

Care: Light prune in early spring when any dead wood should be removed. Enrich annually with garden compost or well rotted manure. Keep well watered in dry periods.

◐ ◑ | ◖ | ❋❋❋ | P2

Clematis 'Elvan'

A late flowering clematis carrying nodding heads of intense violet-purple, loosely striped with creamy-white, in profusion from late summer through until autumn. Of vigorous habit and free flowering, it may be relied upon to produce a remarkable display. Plant as a backdrop to autumnal asters.

Height × spread: Climbing or trailing to 3–3.5m/10–12ft.

Soil: For any well drained but moist soil.

Position: Suitable for planting against a wall, to cover a pergola, trellis, or to climb into a shrub or tree.

Care: Hard prune to ground level in early spring. Enrich annually with garden compost or well rotted manure. Keep well watered in dry periods.

◐◑ | ◑ | ❋❋❋ | P3

Clematis × *eriostemon* 'Hendersonii'

A partially clinging clematis producing hanging flowers of deep violet-blue with yellow-green stamens from midsummer through until autumn. An easy and rewarding plant which is possibly at its best when allowed to scramble at will through the herbaceous border.

Height × spread: Climbing or trailing to 2–2.4m/6–8ft.

Soil: For any well drained but moist soil.

Position: Most effective when planted to climb into a small shrub, when some initial support may be required, or to trail through the border.

Care: Hard prune to ground level in early spring. Enrich annually with garden compost or well rotted manure. Keep well watered in dry periods.

○ ◑ | ◊ | ✳✳✳ | P3

Clematis 'Ernest Markham'

This large flowered hybrid clematis produces flowers of bright magenta-pink of a slightly textured appearance from midsummer through until autumn. Prolific with foliage, it can prove reluctant to flower and should be planted in full sun for best results.

Height × spread: Climbing or trailing to 4.5m/15ft.

Soil: For any well drained but moist soil.

Position: Suitable for planting against a wall, to cover a pergola or trellis, or to climb into a shrub or tree. In shade it is unlikely to flower.

Care: Hard prune to ground level in early spring. Enrich annually with garden compost or well rotted manure. Keep well watered in dry periods.

◯ ◐ ❄❄❄ P3

Clematis 'Etoile de Malicorne'

A distinctive and unusual clematis producing large flowers of lavender-mauve with a deep pink-purple bar in early summer and again, intermittently, in late summer and autumn. An ideal candidate to scramble through a border.

Height × spread: Climbing or trailing to 2m/6ft.

Soil: For any well drained but moist soil.

Position: Suitable for planting against a wall but equally effective when allowed to trail through a border or to reach into the lower branches of a shrub.

Care: Light prune in early spring when any dead wood should be removed. Enrich annually with garden compost or well rotted manure. Keep well watered in dry periods.

◐ ◑ | ◊ | ❄❄❄ | P2

Clematis 'Etoile Rose'

A highly desirable and much sought after late clematis producing long, bell-shaped flowers of deep cherry-pink, paler on the insides, with lighter pink streaks over attractive mid-green foliage from midsummer through to autumn. Inferior crosses may be sold as 'Etoile Rose'.

Height × spread: Climbing or trailing to 3–4.5m/10–15ft.

Soil: For any well drained but moist soil.

Position: Suitable for planting against a wall but possibly at its best when allowed to clothe an evergreen hedge or to climb into a shrub or tree.

Care: Hard prune to ground level in early spring. Enrich annually with garden compost or well rotted manure. Keep well watered in dry periods.

○ ◑ | ◐ | ❄❄❄ | P3

Clematis 'Etoile Violette'

Enjoyed for its mass of deep purple flowers borne in profusion from midsummer through until autumn, this clematis remains deservedly popular. A central eye of cream stamens lifts a flower which might otherwise appear a little dull.

Height × spread: Climbing or trailing to 3–3.5m/10–12ft.

Soil: For any well drained but moist soil.

Position: Suitable for planting against a wall, to cover a pergola or trellis, or to climb through a shrub rose of complementary or contrasting colour.

Care: Hard prune to ground level in early spring. Enrich annually with garden compost or well rotted manure. Keep well watered in dry periods.

◐ ◑ | ◐ | ❋❋❋ | P3

Clematis 'Fireworks'

A large flowered hybrid clematis carrying, as its name suggests, a dramatic and exciting flower of pale violet-mauve with deep magenta-pink bar and an eye of cream stamens touched with traces of pink in early summer. May be container grown given some support.

Height × spread: Climbing or trailing to 2–2.4m/6–8ft.

Soil: For any well drained but moist soil.

Position: Suitable for planting against a wall or to climb into a shrub or tree. May also be sited to cover an obelisk or other free-standing structure.

Care: Light prune in early spring when any dead wood should be removed. Enrich annually with garden compost or well rotted manure. Keep well watered in dry periods.

Clematis florida 'Flore Pleno'

An outstanding clematis noted for its wonderful, double flowers of creamy-white tinged with palest green from early summer until autumn. Unlikely to succeed in anything but the warmest of situations, it may successfully be cultivated as a conservatory plant.

Height × spread: Climbing or trailing to 2–3m/6–10ft.

Soil: For any well drained but moist soil.

Position: Suitable for planting against a warm wall in full sun with protection from cold, drying winds. Intolerant of exposed situations.

Care: Light prune in early spring when any dead wood should be removed. Enrich annually with garden compost or well rotted manure. Keep well watered in dry periods.

◐ ◑ ❊❊❊ (borderline) P2

Clematis florida 'Sieboldii'

A most unusual clematis, the mid to late summer flower of which is often mistaken for that of a passion flower. Creamy-white sepals combine with those of a lustrous purple to form a dome-shaped arrangement. Unlikely to succeed in cold or exposed areas.

Height × spread: Climbing or trailing to 2–3m/6–10ft.

Soil: For any well drained but moist soil.

Position: Suitable for planting against a warm wall in full sun with protection from extremes of cold.

Care: Either light prune in early spring when any dead wood should be removed or hard prune at the same time of year to ground level. Enrich annually with garden compost or well rotted manure. Keep well watered in dry periods.

○ ◐ ❄❄❄ (borderline) P2/3

Clematis forsteri

An evergreen clematis for a sheltered position,
conservatory or cold greenhouse. Scented flowers of
creamy-white with yellowish stamens are produced in
profusion over narrow, tapering leaves in early summer.
Stems are inclined to become tangled and it may,
periodically, be necessary to cut back hard.

Height × spread: Climbing or trailing to 2.4–3.5m/8–12ft.

Soil: For any well drained but moist soil.

Position: In colder areas afford the protection of a wall, against
which it may be planted, in full sun. Intolerant of exposed situations and
cold, drying winds.

Care: Remove unwanted growth after flowering and before
midsummer. Enrich annually with garden compost or well rotted manure.
Keep well watered in dry periods.

| ◯ | ◑ | E | ❋❋ | P1 |

Clematis 'Gipsy Queen'

Flowers of a deep purple with a velvet texture are produced on this vigorous clematis from midsummer through until autumn. This shade of plum-purple looks especially effective when planted with gold or silver foliage such as is to be found on *Choisya ternata* 'Sundance' or *Elaeagnus × ebbingei* 'Limelight'.

Height × spread: Climbing or trailing to 3–3.5m/10–12ft.

Soil: For any well drained but moist soil.

Position: Suitable for planting against a wall, to grow against a pergola, trellis, or similar, or to allow to climb into a shrub or tree.

Care: Hard prune to ground level in early spring. Enrich annually with garden compost or well rotted manure. Keep well watered in dry periods.

○ ◑ | ◐ | ❄❄❄ | P3

Clematis 'Gravetye Beauty'

A late flowering clematis producing rich red flowers opening bell-shaped and gradually unfolding into open stars from midsummer until autumn. Petals in appearance carry a soft sheen and retain their colour throughout the flowering period. Well worth seeking out and not at all difficult in cultivation.

Height × spread: Climbing or trailing to 2–2.4m/6–8ft.

Soil: For any well drained but moist soil.

Position: Ideally suited to climbing into the lower branches of a shrub or tree or to trail through the border.

Care: Hard prune to ground level in early spring. Enrich annually with garden compost or well rotted manure. Keep well watered in dry periods.

○ ◑ | ◐ | ✳✳✳ | P3

Clematis 'Guernsey Cream'

Aptly named 'Guernsey Cream', the depth and richness of the cream flowers appearing in early summer are most apparent when this clematis is placed against a dark background such as, perhaps, a dark leafed holly or deep green yew.

Height × spread: Climbing or trailing to 2m/6ft.

Soil: For any well drained but moist soil.

Position: Suitable for planting against a wall or to climb into a shrub or tree. May also be sited to cover an obelisk or other free-standing structure.

Care: Light prune in early spring when any dead wood should be removed. Enrich annually with garden compost or well rotted manure. Keep well watered in dry periods.

◯ ◑ | 💧 | ✳✳✳ | P2

Clematis 'Hagley Hybrid'

A vigorous and easy clematis producing large, pale mauve-pink flowers in plenty from midsummer, if lightly pruned, and later, into autumn, if hard pruned. Flowers will, particularly when placed in sun, fade rapidly to become somewhat washed out.

Height × spread: Climbing or trailing to 2.4m/8ft.

Soil: For any well drained but moist soil.

Position: Suitable for planting against a wall, to cover a pergola, trellis, or similar, or to climb into a shrub or tree.

Care: Either light prune in early spring when any dead wood should be removed or hard prune at the same time of year to ground level. Enrich annually with garden compost or well rotted manure. Keep well watered in dry periods.

Clematis 'Haku-ôkan'

A recent introduction from Japan, this clematis produces deep violet flowers, the sepals surrounding a central cluster of cream-white stamens, in early summer and again at the start of autumn. The flowers give the appearance of starfish.

Height × spread: Climbing or trailing to 2m/6ft.

Soil: For any well drained but moist soil.

Position: Suitable for planting against a wall or to climb into a shrub or tree. May also be sited to cover an obelisk or other free-standing structure.

Care: Light prune in early spring when any dead wood should be removed. Enrich annually with garden compost or well rotted manure. Keep well watered in dry periods.

◐◑ ⬤ ❄❄❄ P2

Clematis 'Henryi'

One of the oldest large flowered hybrids to remain in cultivation, this clematis produces white flowers with a cream undertone in both midsummer and early autumn. Foliage is somewhat leathery in appearance. Seen here, it complements the silver leaf of *Atriplex halimus*.

Height × spread: Climbing or trailing to 2–3m/6–10ft.

Soil: For any well drained but moist soil.

Position: Suitable for planting against a wall or to climb into a shrub or the lower branches of a tree or to trail through the border.

Care: Light prune in early spring when any dead wood should be removed. Enrich annually with garden compost or well rotted manure. Keep well watered in dry periods.

◐ ◑ | ◊ | ✳✳✳ | P2

Clematis heracleifolia

A semi-herbaceous, non-climbing clematis forming a woody base from which violet-blue flowers and mid-green foliage emerge annually. Flowers, closely resembling those of a hyacinth, appear in late summer. Named forms include *C.h.* var. *davidiana* 'Wyevale' which is, perhaps, superior to the species.

Height × spread: Reaching 1m/3ft.

Soil: For any well drained but moist soil.

Position: For inclusion in the mixed or herbaceous border where it should associate well with other plantings of the late summer.

Care: Hard prune to ground level in early spring. Enrich annually with garden compost or well rotted manure. Keep well watered in dry periods.

○ ◑ | ◐ | ❋❋❋ | P3

Clematis integrifolia

An herbaceous clematis of clump forming habit over which are carried nodding flowers of violet-blue, although the colour may vary, in midsummer. Named forms are numerous and include the white 'Alba', light pink 'Pastel Pink' and the clear blue 'Pastel Blue'.

Height × spread: Trailing with some support to 1m/3ft.

Soil: For any well drained but moist soil.

Position: For inclusion in the mixed or herbaceous border, where it should be supported with pea sticks, or to trail into the lower branches of a small shrub.

Care: Hard prune to ground level in early spring. Enrich annually with garden compost or well rotted manure. Keep well watered in dry periods.

◯ ◑ | ◐ | ❋❋❋ | P3

Clematis integrifolia 'Rosea'

An herbaceous clematis of clump forming habit over which are carried the most charming, nodding flowers in midsummer. Long, twisted sepals of darkest pink, paler on the insides, are ribbed at the base and crimped along the edges. Stamens are of a deep yellow.

Height × spread: Trailing with some support to 60cm/2ft.

Soil: For any well drained but moist soil.

Position: For inclusion in the mixed or herbaceous border, where it should be supported with pea sticks, or simply allowed to trail.

Care: Hard prune to ground level in early spring. Enrich annually with garden compost or well rotted manure. Keep well watered in dry periods.

| ◐ ◑ | ◐ | ❋❋❋ | P3 |

Clematis 'Jackmanii Superba'

An easy, vigorous, free flowering clematis carrying large blue-purple flowers in profusion in mid and late summer. Deservedly popular and widely available. Other named forms may be obtained, most notably 'Jackmanii Alba' and 'Jackmanii Rubra', both producing double blooms from the current season's growth.

Height × spread: Climbing or trailing to 2.4–3m/8–10ft.

Soil: For any well drained but moist soil.

Position: Suitable for planting against a wall, to cover a pergola, trellis, or similar, or to climb into a shrub or tree.

Care: Hard prune to ground level in early spring. Enrich annually with garden compost or well rotted manure. Keep well watered in dry periods.

◐ ◑ | ◊ | ❋❋❋ | P3

Clematis 'John Huxtable'

An excellent, pure white flowered clematis for mid and late summer when it may be relied upon to produce a most worthwhile show. White sepals surround deep cream stamens. Described as a white 'Comtesse de Bouchaud' for similarities of growth and habit. It is unusual to find a white clematis flowering entirely on the current season's growth.

Height × spread: Climbing or trailing to 2–2.4m/6–8ft.

Soil: For any well drained but moist soil.

Position: Suitable for planting against a wall or to climb into a shrub or tree.

Care: Hard prune to ground level in early spring. Enrich annually with garden compost or well rotted manure. Keep well watered in dry periods.

◯ ◑ ◊ ❄❄❄ P3

Clematis × jouiniana 'Praecox'

A non-clinging, late flowering, sub-shrubby clematis forming a woody base from which emerge both foliage and flowers annually. Flowers, perhaps lacking distinction, are off-white with mauve tips and are carried in profusion over large leaves from midsummer until autumn.

Height × spread: Trailing to 2–3m/6–10ft.

Soil: For any well drained but moist soil.

Position: Suitable for trailing through a mixed border or to grow into the lower branches of a shrub. Equally good when placed to scramble down a bank or incline.

Care: Hard prune to ground level in early spring. Enrich annually with garden compost or well rotted manure. Keep well watered in dry periods.

○ ◑ | ◧ | ❄❄❄ | P3

Clematis 'Kakio' (syn. 'Pink Champagne')

A hybrid clematis flowering in the early summer. The cerise-pink flowers, paler towards the centre and possessing an eye of golden stamens, capture an extravagant, fun-loving mood. Seldom seen, well worth acquiring and growing.

Height × spread: Climbing or trailing to 2–2.4m/6–8ft.

Soil: For any well drained but moist soil.

Position: Suitable for planting against a wall, to cover a pergola, trellis, or similar, or to climb into a shrub or tree.

Care: Light prune in early spring when any dead wood should be removed. Enrich annually with garden compost or well rotted manure. Keep well watered in dry periods.

◐ ◑ | ◊ | ✳✳✳ | P2

Clematis 'Kathleen Wheeler'

Flowers of this hybrid clematis open a plummy-mauve
and pleasantly fade as the blooms go over. Overlapping
sepals are grooved, the colour being darker in these areas.
'Kathleen Wheeler' may be relied upon to flower both in
early summer and again at the approach of autumn.

Height × spread: Climbing or trailing to 2.4m/8ft.

Soil: For any well drained but moist soil.

Position: Suitable for planting against a wall or to climb into a shrub
or the lower branches of a tree or to trail through the border.

Care: Light prune in early spring when any dead wood should be
removed. Enrich annually with garden compost or well rotted manure.
Keep well watered in dry periods.

◯ ◖ | ◖ | ❊❊❊ | P2

Clematis 'Kermesina'

A large flowering clematis with rich, crimson-red flowers of velvet texture from midsummer through until autumn. All of the later flowering clematis, and this is no exception, are useful companion plants for shrubs whose flowering season is over.

Height × spread: Climbing or trailing to 3–3.5m/10–12ft.

Soil: For any well drained but moist soil.

Position: Suitable for planting against a wall or to grow against a pergola, trellis, or similar, or to climb into a shrub or tree.

Care: Hard prune to ground level in early spring. Enrich annually with garden compost or well rotted manure. Keep well watered in dry periods.

◐ ◑ ◐ ✻✻✻ P3

Clematis 'Lady Londesborough'

An early hybrid clematis of moderate growth carrying medium size, very pale, silvery mauve-pink flowers in early summer. Producing a pleasing display, the flowers tend to come at once and are therefore over at the same time leaving little to follow.

Height × spread: Climbing or trailing to 1.5–2m/5–6ft.

Soil: For any well drained but moist soil.

Position: Suitable for planting against a wall or to climb into a shrub or the lower branches of a tree or to trail through the border.

Care: Light prune in early spring when any dead wood should be removed. Enrich annually with garden compost or well rotted manure. Keep well watered in dry periods.

○ ◑ | ◗ | ✳✳✳ | P2

Clematis 'Lady Northcliffe'

This large flowered hybrid clematis remains popular not least on account of its long flowering period from early summer until early autumn during which time it is seldom without bloom. Flowers are of a bright lavender-purple, the sepals surrounding stamens of dull cream. Of moderate growth.

Height × spread: Climbing or trailing to 1.5–2m/5–6ft.

Soil: For any well drained but moist soil.

Position: Suitable for planting against a wall or to climb into a shrub or tree. May also be sited to cover an obelisk or other free-standing structure.

Care: Light prune in early spring when any dead wood should be removed. Enrich annually with garden compost or well rotted manure. Keep well watered in dry periods.

○ ◐ | ◊ | ✳✳✳ | P2

Clematis 'Ladybird Johnson'

Trumpet-shaped flowers of a dusky red, the edges of which become tinted purple with age, characterize this late clematis whose cream stamens provide a marked contrast of colour. Flowers from late summer into autumn. An attractive and desirable clematis.

Height × spread: Climbing or trailing to 2–2.4m/6–8ft.

Soil: For any well drained but moist soil.

Position: Suitable for planting against a wall, to climb into a shrub or tree or to trail through the border.

Care: Hard prune to ground level in early spring. Enrich annually with garden compost or well rotted manure. Keep well watered in dry periods.

○ ◑ | ◊ | ✳✳✳ | P3

Clematis 'Lasurstern'

A strong growing clematis producing large flowers of deep mauve-blue, fading in strong sunlight, in early summer and once more, to a lesser extent, in autumn. The second flush of flowers is improved with regular feeding.

Height × spread: Climbing or trailing to 2.4m/8ft.

Soil: For any well drained but moist soil.

Position: Suitable for planting against a wall, to cover a pergola, trellis, or similar, or to climb into a shrub or tree.

Care: Light prune in early spring when any dead wood should be removed. Enrich annually with garden compost or well rotted manure. Keep well watered in dry periods.

◯ ◑ | ◗ | ❊❊❊ | P2

Clematis 'Lincoln Star'

A striking clematis carrying large flowers of deep pink, the margins of each sepal of a paler shade, in early summer and again at the approach of autumn when the flowers are considerably smaller. Unfortunately, 'Lincoln Star' is not a strong grower.

Height × spread: Climbing or trailing to 1.5m/5ft.

Soil: For any well drained but moist soil.

Position: Well suited to climbing into the lower branches of a shrub or to trail through the borders. Alternatively, position at the base of a more vigorous climber.

Care: Light prune in early spring when any dead wood should be removed. Enrich annually with garden compost or well rotted manure. Keep well watered in dry periods.

○ ◑ | ◐ | ❋❋❋ | P2

Clematis 'Little Nell'

An enchanting, small flowered clematis with flowers comprising narrow sepals of white, margined with broad bands of pale pink, surrounding green stamens from midsummer through until early autumn. Possibly at its best when positioned to grow through an early flowering shrub.

Height × **spread:** Climbing or trailing to 3–3.5m/10–12ft.

Soil: For any well drained but moist soil.

Position: Suitable for planting against a wall or to grow against a pergola, trellis, or similar, or to climb into a shrub or tree.

Care: Hard prune to ground level in early spring. Enrich annually with garden compost or well rotted manure. Keep well watered in dry periods.

○ ◑ ◊ ❅❅❅ P3

Clematis 'Lord Nevill'

One of the most intensely blue of all clematis producing
large flowers in early summer and again at the onset of
autumn. A concentration of colour along the veins has the
effect of giving the flowers a somewhat textured
appearance.

Height × spread: Climbing or trailing to 2.4m/8ft.

Soil: For any well drained but moist soil.

Position: Suitable for planting against a wall, to cover a pergola,
trellis, or similar, or to climb into a shrub or tree.

Care: Light prune in early spring when any dead wood should be
removed. Enrich annually with garden compost or well rotted manure.
Keep well watered in dry periods.

◐◑ ◊ ✳✳✳ P2

Clematis 'Louise Rowe'

A particularly appealing and seldom seen double clematis producing flowers of the palest blush pink in the early summer. This clematis would be most effective paired with another large flowered hybrid of contrasting or complementary colour.

Height × spread: Climbing or trailing to 2.4m/8ft.

Soil: For any well drained but moist soil.

Position: Suitable for planting against a wall or to climb into a shrub or the lower branches of a tree or to trail through the border.

Care: Light prune in early spring when any dead wood should be removed. Enrich annually with garden compost or well rotted manure. Keep well watered in dry periods.

○ ◑ | ◊ | ❋❋❋ | P2

Clematis macropetala 'Maidwell Hall'

A spring flowering clematis with leaves of fresh green and carrying somewhat spiky blue flowers which will often produce a second flush in the autumn. Attractive seedheads. Other named forms of *C. macropetala* include the elegant, pure white 'Snowbird'.

Height × spread: Climbing or trailing to 2–2.4m/6–8ft.

Soil: For any well drained but moist soil.

Position: Suitable for planting against a wall, to climb into a shrub or to trail through the border. Best in partial shade but tolerant of sun.

Care: Remove unwanted growth after flowering and before midsummer. Enrich annually with garden compost or well rotted manure. Keep well watered in dry periods.

◐ | ◊ | ❊❊❊ | P1

Clematis macropetala 'Markham's Pink'

A spring flowering clematis with spiky rose-pink flowers, duskier on the reverse, sometimes flowering for a second time in the autumn. Include in a spring border to trail amongst the earliest of perennials to create a different and very pretty effect.

Height × spread: Climbing or trailing to 2–2.4m/6–8ft.

Soil: For any well drained but moist soil.

Position: Suitable for planting against a wall, to climb into a shrub or to trail through the border. Best in partial shade but tolerant of sun.

Care: Remove unwanted growth after flowering and before midsummer. Enrich annually with garden compost or well rotted manure. Keep well watered in dry periods.

◐ ◑ ❄❄❄ P1

Clematis 'Madame Edouard André'

A deep magenta-red clematis flowering from midsummer through until autumn which, whilst fading in strong sunlight, remains an acceptable colour all season. Cream stamens form an effective contrast with the sepals. Of moderate growth, it is perhaps most successful when allowed to find a path through the border.

Height × spread: Climbing or trailing to 2.4m/8ft.

Soil: For any well drained but moist soil.

Position: Suitable for planting against a wall, to climb into a shrub or tree or to trail through the border.

Care: Hard prune to ground level in early spring. Enrich annually with garden compost or well rotted manure. Keep well watered in dry periods.

○ ◑ ◖ | ❋❋❋ | P3

Clematis 'Madame Julia Correvon'

Of all shades of red, the richness of this midsummer to autumn flowering clematis is amongst the best. Clear yellow stamens provide an effective contrast to the sepals which maintain their vibrancy until falling. Reliably flowers over a long period.

Height × spread: Climbing or trailing to 3–3.5m/10–12ft.

Soil: For any well drained but moist soil.

Position: Suitable for planting against a wall or to grow against a pergola, trellis, or similar, or to climb into a shrub or tree.

Care: Hard prune to ground level in early spring. Enrich annually with garden compost or well rotted manure. Keep well watered in dry periods.

○ ◑ | ◗ | ❄❄❄ | P3

Clematis 'Margot Koster'

The sepals of this later flowering clematis are distinctly separate giving the flower something of a gaping appearance. In bloom from midsummer until the onset of autumn, the flowers are of a deep, plummy-purple and are produced in profusion.

Height × spread: Climbing or trailing to 3–3.5m/10–12ft.

Soil: For any well drained but moist soil.

Position: Suitable for planting against a wall or to grow against a pergola, trellis, or similar, or to climb into a shrub or tree.

Care: Hard prune to ground level in early spring. Enrich annually with garden compost or well rotted manure. Keep well watered in dry periods.

◯ ◑ | ◖ | ❄❄❄ | P3

Clematis 'Marie Boisselot' (syn. 'Madame le Coultre')

Possibly one of the most widely grown of all white clematis and valued for the sheer purity of its large flowers from midsummer until the onset of autumn. Hard pruning in the spring will result in later, smaller flowers.

Height × spread: Climbing or trailing to 2.4–3.5m/8–12ft.

Soil: For any well drained but moist soil.

Position: Suitable for planting against a wall, to cover a pergola, trellis, or similar, or to climb into a shrub or tree.

Care: Light prune in early spring when any dead wood should be removed. Enrich annually with garden compost or well rotted manure. Keep well watered in dry periods.

| ○ ◑ | ◓ | ❋❋❋ | P2 |

Clematis 'Mary Rose'

An unusual and highly sought-after clematis carrying small, spiky double flowers of dull amethyst over a prolonged period from midsummer until well into autumn. Especially good when caught by the sun. 'Mary Rose', once established, is prolific in bloom and of vigorous habit.

Height × spread: Climbing or trailing to 3–3.5m/10–12ft.

Soil: For any well drained but moist soil.

Position: Suitable for planting against a wall or to grow against a pergola, trellis, or similar, or to climb into a shrub or tree.

Care: Hard prune to ground level in early spring. Enrich annually with garden compost or well rotted manure. Keep well watered in dry periods.

◐ ◑ | ◗ | ✳✳✳ | P3

Clematis 'Maureen'

An attractive and easily grown clematis which deserves to be more widely cultivated. In appearance the flowers, consisting of deep purple-red sepals and cream stamens, have a marked textural quality. Most often in bloom from early summer through until autumn depending on the method of pruning adopted.

Height × spread: Climbing or trailing to 2m/6ft.

Soil: For any well drained but moist soil.

Position: Suitable for planting against a wall, to climb into a shrub or tree or to trail through the border.

Care: Either light prune in early spring when any dead wood should be removed or hard prune at the same time of year to ground level. Enrich annually with garden compost or well rotted manure. Keep watered in dry periods.

◑ ◐ | ◊ | ❋❋❋ | P2/3

Clematis 'Miss Bateman'

Flowers of this early summer clematis are of a translucent white with the appearance of being overlaid with a creamy bar. Most effective when placed against a deeply coloured background as is shown here where the clematis is planted to grow through a wine-red *Cotinus*.

Height × **spread:** Climbing or trailing to 2m/6ft.

Soil: For any well drained but moist soil.

Position: Suitable for planting against a wall or to climb into a shrub or the lower branches of a tree or to trail through the border.

Care: Light prune in early spring when any dead wood should be removed. Enrich annually with garden compost or well rotted manure. Keep well watered in dry periods.

◯◑ ⬤ ❄❄❄ P2

Flowering first in early summer and again in late summer, this clematis has flowers of a very pale mauve-pink which, in appearance, have a faint sheen. Sepals are arranged most often in two layers, unequally disposed.

Height × spread: Climbing or trailing to 2m/6ft.

Soil: For any well drained but moist soil.

Position: Suitable for planting against a wall or to climb into a shrub or the lower branches of a tree or to trail through the border.

Care: Light prune in early spring when any dead wood should be removed. Enrich annually with garden compost or well rotted manure. Keep well watered in dry periods.

○ ◑ | ◐ | ❋❋❋ | P2

Clematis montana

A spring flowering clematis of vigorous habit with variable white, vanilla scented flowers with pale cream stamens. Various pink forms are often wrongly referred to simply as *C. montana*; they are, in fact, named varieties. All are easy in cultivation.

Height × spread: Climbing or trailing to 6–9m/20–30ft or more.

Soil: For any well drained but moist soil.

Position: Suitable for planting against a wall, for a pergola, to mask an unsightly building or to grow into a tree. Requires strong support.

Care: Remove unwanted growth after flowering and before midsummer. Enrich annually with garden compost or well rotted manure. Keep well watered in dry periods. Will usually withstand hard pruning to curtail an excess of growth.

○ ◑ | ◐ | ✳✳✳ | P1

Clematis montana 'Elizabeth'

A spring flowering clematis of vigorous habit with slightly cupped, clear pink, vanilla scented flowers. Young leaves are attractively tinted purple. Constant attention is required if stems are not to become a twisted mass.

Height × spread: Climbing or trailing to 6–9m/20–30ft or more.

Soil: For any well drained but moist soil.

Position: Suitable for planting against a wall, for a pergola, to mask an unsightly building or to grow into a tree. Requires strong support.

Care: Remove unwanted growth after flowering and before midsummer. Enrich annually with garden compost or well rotted manure. Keep well watered in dry periods. Will usually withstand hard pruning to curtail an excess of growth.

◑◐ ◊ ❋❋❋ P1

Clematis montana 'Rubens'

A spring flowering clematis of robust, vigorous habit. Vanilla scented flowers are somewhat variable but should be of a soft mauve-pink. Young leaves, as with *C. montana* 'Elizabeth', are tinted purple.

Height × **spread:** Climbing or trailing to 6–9m/20–30ft or more.

Soil: For any well drained but moist soil.

Position: Suitable for planting against a wall, for a pergola, to mask an unsightly building or to grow into a tree. Ensure that any host is of sufficient strength to support the weight of the clematis.

Care: Remove unwanted growth after flowering and before midsummer. Enrich annually with garden compost or well rotted manure. Keep well watered in dry periods. Will usually withstand hard pruning to curtail an excess of growth.

◐ ◑ | ◊ | ✳✳✳ | P1

Clematis montana 'Tetrarose'

A spring flowering clematis, less vigorous in habit than the species, with bowl-shaped, deep rose-pink flowers which carry a scent reminiscent of cedarwood. Leaves are of an attractive bronze-green.

Height × spread: Climbing or trailing to 6m/20ft or more.

Soil: For any well drained but moist soil.

Position: Suitable for planting against a wall, for a pergola, to mask an unsightly building or to grow into a tree. Ensure that any host is of sufficient strength to support the weight of the clematis.

Care: Remove unwanted growth after flowering and before midsummer. Enrich annually with garden compost or well rotted manure. Keep well watered in dry periods. Will usually withstand hard pruning to curtail an excess of growth.

○ ◑ ◐ | ✳✳✳ | P1

Clematis montana 'Warwickshire Rose'

A spring flowering clematis of vigorous habit. Flowers comprise four sepals, deep rose-pink in bud, opening to variable shades of pink, most often darker at the margins. Stamens are creamy-yellow. Young leaves are a deep bronze.

Height × spread: Climbing or trailing to 6–9m/20–30ft or more.

Soil: For any well drained but moist soil.

Position: Suitable for planting against a wall, for a pergola, to mask an unsightly building or to grow into a tree. Ensure that any host is of sufficient strength to support the weight of the clematis.

Care: Remove unwanted growth after flowering and before midsummer. Enrich annually with garden compost or well rotted manure. Keep well watered in dry periods. Will usually withstand hard pruning to curtail an excess of growth.

○ ◑ | ◗ | ❋❋❋ | P1

Clematis 'Mrs. Cholmondeley'

Flowering time for this attractive clematis with flowers of palest violet-blue depends on pruning. Light pruning results in flowers on a vigorous plant from late spring until the onset of autumn. Hard pruning restricts growth with flowering delayed until midsummer.

Height × spread: Climbing to 6m/20ft.

Soil: For any well drained but moist soil.

Position: Suitable for planting against a wall, to cover a pergola, trellis, or similar, or to climb into a shrub or tree.

Care: Either light prune in early spring when any dead wood should be removed or hard prune at the same time of year to ground level. Enrich annually with garden compost or well rotted manure. Keep well watered in dry periods.

| ◐ ◑ | ◓ | ✳✳✳ | P2/3 |

Clematis 'Mrs. George Jackman'

Not at all dissimilar to *C.* 'Marie Boisselot', the flowers of 'Mrs. George Jackman', flowering in early summer and again at the start of autumn, are creamier and inclined to be a little smaller. The stamens are dome-shaped.

Height × spread: Climbing or trailing to 2.4m/8ft.

Soil: For any well drained but moist soil.

Position: Suitable for planting against a wall, to cover a pergola, trellis, or similar, or to climb into a shrub or tree.

Care: Light prune in early spring when any dead wood should be removed. Enrich annually with garden compost or well rotted manure. Keep well watered in dry periods.

Clematis 'Mrs. P.B. Truax'

This early summer flowering clematis is noted for its unusual shape of tapering sepals of pale mauve-blue, reflexed at the tips. Both sepals and creamy stamens give the appearance of silk. Very occasionally a few flowers are produced in autumn.

Height × spread: Climbing or trailing to 2m/6ft.

Soil: For any well drained but moist soil.

Position: Suitable for planting against a wall, to climb into a shrub or tree or trail through the border.

Care: Light prune in early spring when any dead wood should be removed. Enrich annually with garden compost or well rotted manure. Keep well watered in dry periods.

○ ◑ | ◊ | ❋❋❋ | P2

Clematis 'Nelly Moser'

One of the best known of all large flowered hybrid clematis which may be relied upon for an eye-catching display in early summer and again at the onset of autumn. Flowers, rapidly fading in sunlight, are of a rose-mauve with a broad, central bar of carmine.

Height × spread: Climbing or trailing to 2–3m/6–10ft.

Soil: For any well drained but moist soil.

Position: Suitable for planting against a wall, to cover a pergola, trellis, or similar, or to climb into a shrub or tree.

Care: Light prune in early spring when any dead wood should be removed. Enrich annually with garden compost or well rotted manure. Keep well watered in dry periods.

◑ ◐ | ◊ | ✳✳✳ | P2

Clematis 'Niobe'

Ruby-red flowers are carried on this clematis according to when pruning takes place. Light pruning results in flowers from early summer until the autumn. Hard pruning restricts the moderate growth further with flowers appearing in late summer.

Height × spread: Climbing or trailing to 2.4m/8ft.

Soil: For any well drained but moist soil.

Position: Suitable for planting against a wall, to cover a pergola, trellis, or similar, or to climb into a shrub or tree.

Care: Either light prune in early spring when any dead wood should be removed or hard prune at the same time of year to ground level. Enrich annually with garden compost or well rotted manure. Keep well watered in dry periods.

◐◑ ◊ ❋❋❋ P2/3

Clematis orientalis

Nodding, hanging bell-flowers of deep butter-yellow typify this clematis which is in flower almost continuously from midsummer through until autumn. Foliage is of a fresh green. Seedheads, which remain well into winter, are an additional attraction. 'Bill Mackenzie' is a named form.

Height × spread: Climbing to 3–7.5m/10–25ft.

Soil: For any well drained but moist soil.

Position: Suitable for planting against a wall or to grow against a pergola, trellis, or similar, or to climb into a shrub or tree.

Care: Hard prune to ground level in early spring. Enrich annually with garden compost or well rotted manure. Keep well watered in dry periods.

◯ ◑ ◖ | ❅❅❅ | P3

Clematis 'Perle d'Azur'

Deservedly popular, this clematis is enjoyed for its profusion of blue-mauve flowers which appear in a mass from midsummer until the onset of autumn. Sepals, corrugated in appearance, are in contrast to small, pale green stamens. New plants may suffer from wilt but will almost certainly recover.

Height × spread: Climbing to 3–4.5m/10–15ft.

Soil: For any well drained but moist soil.

Position: Suitable for planting against a wall or to grow against a pergola, trellis, or similar, or to climb into a shrub or tree.

Care: Hard prune to ground level in early spring. Enrich annually with garden compost or well rotted manure. Keep well watered in dry periods.

◐ ◑ | ◐ | ❄❄❄ | P3

Clematis 'Polish Spirit'

A late flowering clematis producing small flowers of
violet-blue with a magenta bar in late summer. Most
effective when shown against a contrasting background,
such as the golden leaves of *Philadelphus coronarius*
'Aureus'.

Height × spread: Climbing or trailing to 2m/6ft.

Soil: For any well drained but moist soil.

Position: Suitable for planting against a wall, to climb into a shrub or
tree or to trail through the border. May also be sited to cover an obelisk
or other free-standing structure.

Care: Hard prune to ground level in early spring. Enrich annually with
garden compost or well rotted manure. Keep well watered in dry
periods.

◐ ◑ | ◐ | ❄❄❄ | P3

Not dissimilar in appearance to *C.* 'Perle d'Azur', this clematis carries flowers of intense violet-mauve with deeper markings from midsummer through until autumn although seldom in a mass. Probably at its best when allowed to scramble through a shrub such as the dark leafed *Berberis* shown here.

Height × **spread:** Climbing or trailing to 2m/6ft.

Soil: For any well drained but moist soil.

Position: Suitable for planting against a wall, to climb into a shrub or tree or to trail through the border.

Care: Hard prune to ground level in early spring. Enrich annually with garden compost or well rotted manure. Keep well watered in dry periods.

◐ ◐ ◖ ❀❀❀ P3

Clematis 'Princess of Wales'

This late flowering clematis carries trumpet-shaped flowers of vivid, deep pink, paling at the margins, in late summer and early autumn. Introduced in 1984 and named for the late Diana, Princess of Wales, it is a cross between *C.* 'Bees Jubilee' and *C. texensis*.

Height × spread: Climbing or trailing to 2–2.4m/6–8ft.

Soil: For any well drained but moist soil.

Position: Suitable for planting against a wall, to climb into a shrub or tree or to trail through the border where, on account of its habit, it is easily managed.

Care: Hard prune to ground level in early spring. Enrich annually with garden compost or well rotted manure. Keep well watered in dry periods.

○ ◑	◗	✳✳✳	P3

Clematis 'Proteus'

Double mauve-pink flowers of this clematis, not dissimilar
to a double peony, are carried principally in early summer
and again at the start of autumn. Often slow to establish, it
is of moderate growth.

Height × **spread:** Climbing or trailing to 2m/6ft.

Soil: For any well drained but moist soil.

Position: Suitable for planting against a wall or to climb into a shrub
or the lower branches of a tree or to trail through the border.

Care: Light prune in early spring when any dead wood should be
removed. Enrich annually with garden compost or well rotted manure.
Keep well watered in dry periods.

○ ◑ | ◐ | ❋❋❋ | P2

An herbaceous perennial clematis whose flowers, appearing starry in a mass in midsummer, are somewhat unreliable with regard to scent, some forms being entirely scentless. Named varieties include 'Peveril' and 'Purpurea'.

Height × spread: Trailing with some support to 1–2m/3–6ft.

Soil: For any well drained but moist soil.

Position: Suitable for a mixed border in an open situation. Use pea sticks to provide some necessary support or intermix with other plantings.

Care: Hard prune to ground level in early spring. Enrich annually with garden compost or well rotted manure. Keep well watered in dry periods.

◯ ◐ | ◌ | ✳✳✳ | P3

Clematis rehderiana

If left unpruned, then this clematis will reach 6m/20ft or more becoming a tangled mass of twining stems. Pruned, it forms an attractive climber of some 3m/10ft producing scented, nodding bell flowers of creamy-yellow in late summer and at the commencement of autumn.

Height × spread: Climbing to 6m/20ft if left unpruned.

Soil: For any well drained but moist soil.

Position: Suitable for planting against a wall or to grow against a pergola, trellis, or similar, or to climb into a shrub or tree.

Care: Hard prune to ground level in early spring. Enrich annually with garden compost or well rotted manure. Keep well watered in dry periods.

| ◯ ◑ | ◐ | ✳✳✳ | P3 |

Clematis 'Rouge Cardinal'

The velvet-red flowers of this late summer clematis unfortunately fade rapidly to an unremarkable beetroot shade. Furthermore, 'Rouge Cardinal' is generally reluctant to flower. Possibly at best when allowed to roam through a mixed border for heightened interest.

Height × spread: Climbing or trailing to 2m/6ft.

Soil: For any well drained but moist soil.

Position: Suitable for planting against a wall or to climb into a shrub or tree. May also be sited to cover an obelisk or other free-standing structure.

Care: Hard prune to ground level in early spring. Enrich annually with garden compost or well rotted manure. Keep well watered in dry periods. Apply a thick mulch in winter in cold areas for added protection.

○ ◑ | ◑ | ❄❄❄ | P3

Clematis 'Royal Velours'

Aptly named, the flowers of this mid to late summer clematis possess a sheen which is readily suggestive of velvet. Overlapping sepals open to a deep wine-red tinged with purple, a colour to which it later fades. Wonderful when allowed to cavort through a host shrub.

Height × spread: Climbing or trailing to 3–3.5m/10–12ft.

Soil: For any well drained but moist soil.

Position: Suitable for planting against a wall or to grow against a pergola, trellis, or similar, or to climb into a shrub or tree.

Care: Hard prune to ground level in early spring. Enrich annually with garden compost or well rotted manure. Keep well watered in dry periods.

◯◑ ◊ ✳✳✳ P3

Clematis 'Royalty'

The double flowers of this clematis are followed in autumn by single ones. Sepals of an intense violet-purple, flushed with magenta, are set off by an eye of cream stamens. 'Royalty', introduced in 1973, closely resembles *C.* 'Susan Allsop'.

Height × spread: Climbing or trailing to 2.4m/8ft.

Soil: For any well drained but moist soil.

Position: Suitable for planting against a wall or to climb into a shrub or the lower branches of a tree or to trail through the border.

Care: Light prune in early spring when any dead wood should be removed. Enrich annually with garden compost or well rotted manure. Keep well watered in dry periods.

| ◯ ◑ | ◊ | ❄❄❄ | P2 |

Clematis 'Sir Trevor Lawrence'

Relatively uncommon, this clematis has tulip-shaped flowers of a brilliant crimson shaded light violet at the outer edges. Sepals are inclined to roll over at the tips to give a somewhat furled appearance. Named after a former president of the Royal Horticultural Society.

Height × spread: Climbing or trailing to 2–2.4m/6–8ft.

Soil: For any well drained but moist soil.

Position: Suitable for planting against a wall, to climb into a shrub or tree or to trail through the border.

Care: Hard prune to ground level in early spring. Enrich annually with garden compost or well rotted manure. Keep well watered in dry periods.

◐◑ ◊ ❄❄❄ P3

Instantly recognizable on account of its being widely grown, this clematis is noted for its bright, buttercup-yellow, nodding flowers, although the exact shade will vary from plant to plant. Flowering from late summer until autumn, flowers are followed with long lasting seedheads.

Height × spread: Climbing or trailing to 3–4.5m/10–15ft.

Soil: For any well drained but moist soil.

Position: Suitable for planting against a wall or to grow against a pergola, trellis, or similar, or to climb into a shrub or tree.

Care: Hard prune to ground level in early spring. Enrich annually with garden compost or well rotted manure. Keep well watered in dry periods.

○ ◑ │ ◐ │ ❅❅❅ │ P3

Clematis 'The President'

After more than a century the popularity of this easy clematis remains undiminished. Deep, purple to violet-blue flowers from early summer through until autumn are accompanied with bold stamens and foliage which, when young, is bronze-tinted. One of very few continuously flowering clematis.

Height × spread: Climbing or trailing to 2–3m/6–10ft.

Soil: For any well drained but moist soil.

Position: Suitable for planting against a wall, to cover a pergola, trellis, or similar, or to climb into a shrub or tree.

Care: Light prune in early spring when any dead wood should be removed. Enrich annually with garden compost or well rotted manure. Keep well watered in dry periods.

◐ ◑ | ◐ | ❄❄❄ | P2

Clematis × *triternata* 'Rubro-marginata'

A seldom seen late flowering clematis which deserves to be more widely appreciated. Small, dusky-pink flowers, appearing in late summer and autumn, are shaded pinky-red and white, are of cruciform shape and possess prominent green stamens. Some scent although generally faint.

Height × spread: Climbing to 4.5–6m/15–20ft.

Soil: For any well drained but moist soil.

Position: Suitable for planting against a wall or to grow against a pergola, trellis, or similar, or to climb into a shrub or tree.

Care: Hard prune to ground level in early spring. Enrich annually with garden compost or well rotted manure. Keep well watered in dry periods.

| ○ ◑ | ◐ | ❋❋❋ | P3 |

Clematis 'Ville de Lyon'

Although growing in rather a sparse manner, this clematis remains of vigorous habit and continues to be a popular choice. Flowers, carried virtually from late spring until autumn, depending on the method of pruning, are of deep carmine, paler towards the centre.

Height × spread: Climbing to 3–9m/10–30ft.

Soil: For any well drained but moist soil.

Position: Suitable for planting against a wall, to cover a pergola, trellis, or similar, or to climb into a shrub or tree.

Care: Either light prune in early spring when any dead wood should be removed or hard prune at the same time of year to ground level. Enrich annually with garden compost or well rotted manure. Keep well watered in dry periods.

○ ◑ | ◊ | ✻✻✻ | P2/3

Clematis 'Vino'

Most appropriately named, this hybrid clematis has large flowers in early summer of a rich, full-bodied, magenta-red. Pale golden stamens provide an effective contrast. Seldom seen, it is well worth seeking out from specialist nurseries.

Height × spread: Climbing or trailing to 2–2.4m/6–8ft.

Soil: For any well drained but moist soil.

Position: Suitable for planting against a wall, to cover a pergola, trellis, or similar, or to climb into a shrub or tree.

Care: Light prune in early spring when any dead wood should be removed. Enrich annually with garden compost or well rotted manure. Keep well watered in dry periods.

Clematis viorna

An unusual species clematis producing urn-shaped flowers distinguished by recurving sepals in shades of red-purple tipped in creamy-white. Flowers appear in late summer and are followed with large, attractive seedheads. *C. viorna* tends to die back to ground level in winter.

Height × spread: Climbing or trailing to 2.4m/8ft.

Soil: For any well drained but moist soil.

Position: Suitable for planting against a wall, to climb into a shrub or tree or to trail through the border. Best in a warm, sunny situation.

Care: Hard prune to ground level in early spring. Enrich annually with garden compost or well rotted manure. Keep well watered in dry periods.

◯ ◐ ❄❄❄ P3

Clematis viticella 'Purpurea Plena Elegans'

This late flowering clematis is noted for its fully double flowers of a rich red-purple which are produced in profusion from midsummer until early autumn. It is of as vigorous habit as it is free flowering.

Height × spread: Climbing or trailing to 3–3.5m/10–12ft.

Soil: For any well drained but moist soil.

Position: Suitable for planting against a wall, to climb into a shrub, such as *Callicarpa bodinieri* var. *giraldii* with whose berries it associates well, or tree, or to trail through a border.

Care: Hard prune to ground level in early spring. Enrich annually with garden compost or well rotted manure. Keep well watered in dry periods.

○ ◑ | ◖ | ✳✳✳ | P3

Clematis 'W.E. Gladstone'

Flowers of this striking hybrid are of an exceptional size and appear from midsummer through until the early autumn depending on the method of pruning adopted. Overlapping sepals are of lavender-blue arranged around a central eye of stamens.

Height × spread: Climbing to 3.5m/12ft.

Soil: For any well drained but moist soil.

Position: Suitable for planting against a wall, to cover a pergola, trellis, or similar, or to climb into a shrub or tree.

Care: Either light prune in early spring when any dead wood should be removed or hard prune at the same time of year to ground level. Enrich annually with garden compost or well rotted manure. Keep well watered in dry periods.

◐ ◑ | ◊ | ❄❄❄ | P2/3

2.
CLIMBERS

Actinidia kolomikta

Dark green leaves prominently marked with pink and white variegation, as though splashed at random with a paint brush, are the principal feature of this interesting climber. Scented white flowers are carried in early summer to be followed on female plants with fruits. New plants should be given protection from cats who are attracted to the stems.

Height × spread: Climbing to 5m/16ft or more.

Soil: For well drained, fertile soil which does not dry out.

Position: Best grown against a warm, sheltered wall in full sun.

Care: When the allotted space is covered, shorten growth back in early winter.

◖ ◊ ✳✳✳

Deep wine-red flowers, somewhat textured in appearance, open from tightly formed, creamy-yellow buds in spring. These are susceptible to, and may be damaged by, late frosts. The semi-evergreen foliage of this climber is of an attractive light green, very often concealing the heavily scented flowers. For autumn fruits plant male and female clones together to effect pollination. Twining stems require wires for support.

Height × **spread:** Climbing to 9m/30ft or more.

Soil: For well drained, fertile soil which does not dry out.

Position: Best grown against a warm, sheltered wall in full sun.

Care: New stems should be tied in regularly to supports. Remove any dead or weak growth in spring.

◖ ◊ Semi-E ❋❋❋

116

Aristolochia durior: Dutchman's pipe

Grown largely for the extraordinary flower which, in appearance, resembles a curving pipe, hence the common name, and which is carried over handsome, heart-shaped leaves. The intriguing flowers of this climber appear, most often in pairs, in early summer. Twining stems require wires for support.

Height × spread: Climbing to 9m/30ft or more.

Soil: For well drained, fertile soil which does not dry out.

Position: Grow against a wall, to cover a pergola, arch or trellis. An effective green column can be achieved by training *Aristolochia* around a pole or post. For sun or partial shade.

Care: New stems should be tied in regularly to supports. Remove any dead, weak or unwanted growth in spring.

○ ◑ │ ◊ │ ❋❋❋

An exciting, frost hardy climber producing striking flowers of a soft orange-red over veined and toothed leaves, downy on the undersides, in late summer and autumn. Campsis makes an excellent companion plant for some of the late flowering clematis with which it may share a host.

Height × spread: Climbing to 9m/30ft or more.

Soil: For well drained soil which does not dry out. Will thrive in poor conditions where excess growth will be discouraged.

Position: Best grown against a warm, sheltered wall in full sun. Also suitable to cover a pergola, arch or trellis.

Care: To promote flowers it may be advisable to prune back the previous summer's growth in the spring.

Cobaea scandens: Cathedral bell

Originating in Mexico, this frost tender climber is probably best treated in cold areas as an annual when it may readily be grown each year from seed. Twining stems carry somewhat short bells of mauve-purple in summer through into autumn. Also available is a lovely white form, *C. scandens* f. *alba*.

Height × spread: Climbing to 2–3m/6–10ft or more when grown as an annual.

Soil: For well drained, fertile soil which does not dry out.

Position: Best grown against a warm, sheltered wall in full sun. Also suitable to cover a pergola, arch or trellis. Alternatively, well suited to pot cultivation given some support.

Care: Pinch out growing tips during the season to encourage bushy growth.

◖ ◊ ❊

119

Convolvulus althaeoides: Bindweed

Of trailing rather than climbing habit, this frost hardy, herbaceous climber is valued for its attractive, finely cut silver foliage as well as for its very pretty, trumpet-shaped, cerise-pink flowers of satiny texture which appear throughout the summer. Effective when encouraged to scramble over a low wall or among other plantings.

Height × spread: Trailing to 1m/3ft or more.

Soil: For well drained, fertile soil which does not dry out.

Position: For an open, sunny site where it will, with support, climb to around 1m/3ft. Otherwise allow to trail.

Care: Cut hard back each spring. In cold areas apply a mulch over winter for added protection.

○ ◊ ❄❄

Eccremocarpus scaber: Chilean glory vine

This perennial, frost tender climber is, in colder areas, most frequently treated as an annual when it may easily be grown each year from seed. Orange-yellow flowers of long, tubular shape are produced over a prolonged period throughout summer and autumn. Climbs by means of leaf tendrils. For red flowers, grow *E. scaber coccineus*.

Height × spread: Climbing to 4m/13ft or more.

Soil: For well drained, fertile soil which does not dry out.

Position: Grow against a wall, to cover a pergola, arch or trellis. Best in full sun.

Care: In warmer areas cut back hard each spring. Apply a mulch over winter for added protection. Otherwise raise from seed annually.

◯ ◊ ✳

121

Hedera canariensis 'Gloire de Marengo': Ivy

Variegated leaves are the principal attraction of this climbing, evergreen ivy. Broad, irregular margins of creamy-white surround leaves of deep green tinged with grey. These may, in cold winters, suffer from frost and wind damage. May also be cultivated as a house plant. For a smaller leafed ivy, grow *H. helix* 'Goldheart'.

Height × spread: Climbing to 4.5m/15ft or more.

Soil: For well drained, fertile soil. Tolerant of dry conditions.

Position: Grow against a wall, to cover a pergola, arch or trellis or to conceal an unsightly building. Succeeds in sun or partial shade.

Care: No routine pruning is required. Cut back excessive growth in early summer. Remove any stems which do not contain variegation.

◐ ◑ | ◊ | E | ❄❄

Hedera colchica 'Sulphur Heart': Paddy's pride

Brilliantly variegated, evergreen leaves of acid green, generously splashed in the centre somewhat irregularly with a sulphureous yellow, are excellent for lightening a gloomy area. As with most ivies, this climber supports itself by means of stem-roots. A smaller growing, less vigorous, prettily-shaped ivy for any situation is *H. helix* 'Cristata'.

Height × spread: Climbing to 4.5m/15ft or more.

Soil: For well drained, fertile soil. Tolerant of dry conditions.

Position: Grow against a wall, to cover a pergola, arch or trellis or to conceal an unsightly building. Succeeds in sun or partial shade.

Care: No routine pruning is required. Cut back excessive growth in early summer. Remove any stems which do not contain variegation.

◐ ◑ | ◊ | E | ❋❋❋

Hedera helix 'Angularis Aurea': Ivy

The advantage of this evergreen climbing ivy is that the yellow variegated leaves will not scorch if exposed to too much sunlight. However, only exposed leaves are likely to colour and the degree to which they will do so will vary. In some case the whole leaf will be yellow, in others a part, whilst in others no more than the veining.

Height × spread: Climbing to 2.7m/9ft or more.

Soil: For well drained, fertile soil. Tolerant of dry conditions.

Position: Grow against a wall, to cover a pergola, arch or trellis or to form an effective yellow-green column by training around a pole or post. Succeeds in sun or partial shade.

Care: No routine pruning is required. Cut back excessive growth in early summer. Remove any stems which do not contain variegation.

◯ ◑ │ ◊ │ E │ ✳✳✳

Hedera helix 'Buttercup': Ivy

Of all variegated forms of climbing ivy, the evergreen 'Buttercup' has widespread appeal. Lime-yellow leaves are uniformly variegated but must be in full sun and light to remain so. Where grown in shade the leaves will revert to green. This is a good form for the smaller garden or to grow where space is restricted.

Height × spread: Climbing to 2.7m/9ft or more.

Soil: For well drained, fertile soil. Tolerant of dry conditions.

Position: Grow against a wall, to cover a pergola, arch or trellis or to form an effective yellow column by training around a pole or post. Best in full sun.

Care: No routine pruning is required. Cut back excessive growth in early summer. Remove any stems which do not contain variegation.

○ ◊ E ✳✳✳

Hedera helix 'Glacier': Ivy

Where a cool, light background is required to other plantings, then this climbing, evergreen ivy must rank as a worthy candidate. Of vigorous habit, leaves are of a leaden green and grey edged irregularly with broad margins of creamy-white. In some instances this extends across the whole leaf.

Height × spread: Climbing to 4.5m/15ft or more.

Soil: For well drained, fertile soil. Tolerant of dry conditions.

Position: Grow against a wall, to cover a pergola, arch or trellis or to conceal an unsightly building. Succeeds in sun or partial shade.

Care: No routine pruning is required. Cut back excessive growth in early summer. Remove any stems which do not contain variegation.

◐ ◑ | ◊ | E | ❋❋❋

Humulus lupulus 'Aureus': Golden hop

Much space is required for this vigorous foliage climber which extends itself by means of long, twining stems upon which are carried somewhat acid, yellow-green leaves, yellower when positioned in full sun. Added interest is the development of trusses of golden hops in the autumn.

Height × spread: Climbing to 6m/20ft or more.

Soil: For well drained, fertile soil which does not dry out.

Position: Grow against a wall, to cover a pergola, arch or trellis or to conceal in season an unsightly building.

Care: Cut back all stems to ground level after leaf fall. This may be done in late autumn or early spring at which point divisions may be made.

| ○ ◑ | ◊ | ❋❋❋ |

Hydrangea anomala petiolaris: Climbing hydrangea

Use this self-clinging hydrangea to clothe the wall of a house where it will, given time, for it is often slow to establish, form a covering of handsome leaves and carry large, creamy-green flowerheads in early summer.

Height × spread: Climbing to 9m/30ft or more.

Soil: For moisture retentive soil but will tolerate normal, free draining conditions.

Position: Grow against a wall, to cover a pergola, arch or trellis or to conceal in season an unsightly building. Suitable for a shady aspect as well as a sunny one.

Care: Shorten back any unwanted growth in the late summer once the flowering period is over.

○ ◑ ● | ◊ | ❄❄❄

Ipomoea indica: Morning glory/Blue dawn flower

A splendid and exotic-looking, frost tender climber with wide funnel-type flowers of violet-purple throughout the summer and well into autumn. Treat as an annual or, in warmer areas, a short-lived perennial. Flowers open with the morning sun and, as a general rule, fade by midday giving rise to the common name of Morning glory.

Height × spread: Climbing to 4.5m/15ft or more.

Soil: For well drained, fertile soil which does not dry out.

Position: Best grown against a warm, sheltered wall in full sun or in a cool conservatory or glasshouse.

Care: Tie in twining stems to supports.

◐ ◊ ❄

Jasminum officinale: Jasmine

Apart from delighting with its clusters of white trumpet flowers, this vigorous climber will intoxicate with the fragrance of its perfume. Long in cultivation, this jasmine should be afforded plenty of space when it will flower most freely throughout the summer. Attractive foliage is of a darkish green. Support is required for twining stems.

Height × spread: Climbing to 7m/23ft or more.

Soil: For well drained, fertile soil which does not dry out.

Position: Grow against a wall, to cover a pergola, arch or trellis. Succeeds best in full sun.

Care: No routine pruning is required. Cut out old stems and any excess of growth after flowering. New shoots should be tied in regularly to supports.

○ ◊ ❋❋❋

Jasminum polyanthum: Jasmine

Less vigorous than *J. officinale*, this frost hardy climber needs the shelter of a warm wall to flourish in all but the warmest of areas. It may, though, be cultivated in a cool conservatory or glasshouse. Delicate white, heavily scented flowers, pink in bud, are carried over attractive, mid-green foliage throughout the summer.

Height × spread: Climbing to 5m/16ft or more.

Soil: For well drained, fertile soil which does not dry out.

Position: Grow against a wall, to cover a pergola, arch or trellis. Succeeds best in full sun.

Care: No routine pruning is required. Cut out old stems and any excess of growth after flowering. New shoots should be tied in regularly to supports.

Lapageria rosea: Chilean bellflower

An evergreen, frost tender climber displaying heart-shaped leaves against which are shown off beautiful, waxy, crimson-pink, bell-shaped flowers in summer. Not the easiest of plants, it is well worth seeking out and positioning where it will flourish.

Height × spread: Climbing to 2m/6ft or more.

Soil: For well drained, humus-rich, lime free soil which does not dry out.

Position: Outside the warmest of areas, this is a plant for a conservatory or glasshouse where it demands a warm, moist atmosphere and a shady situation.

Care: New stems should be tied in regularly to supports. Remove any dead or weak growth in spring.

◑ ◊ E LH ❋

Often referred to as the everlasting pea, this robust and easy climber will enliven a dark background for the greater part of the summer when it produces a succession of pea-like flowers in shades of pink and magenta. Complement it with one of the large flowered hybrid clematis.

Height × **spread:** Climbing to 1.5m/5ft or more.

Soil: For well drained, fertile soil which does not dry out.

Position: Grow against a wall, to cover a pergola, arch or trellis or to form an effective flowering column by training around a pole or post. Best in sun.

Care: Cut old stems to ground level in late autumn or early spring. Water well during dry periods.

◖	◊	❋❋❋

Lathyrus latifolius 'White Pearl': Perennial pea

An excellent white form of the perennial pea. This robust and easy climber carries pure white, pea-like flowers borne in succession throughout the summer. Reliably good to flower, it is well suited to being included in almost any planting scheme. Particularly effective against a dark background.

Height × spread: Climbing to 2m/6ft or more.

Soil: For well drained, fertile soil which does not dry out.

Position: Grow against a wall, to cover a pergola, arch or trellis or to form an effective flowering column by training around a pole or post. Best in sun.

Care: Cut old stems to ground level in late autumn or early spring. Water well during dry periods.

◯ ◊ ✼✼✼

Lathyrus rotundifolius

An unusual perennial climber which is seldom seen and deserves to be grown more widely. The pea-like flowers, borne in profusion throughout the midsummer, are set off by pleasant leaves of light green. Flower colour is best described as brick-red. Supports itself by means of leaf tendrils. Occasionally self-sown seedlings are to be found around the parent plant.

Height × spread: Climbing to 2m/6ft or more.

Soil: For well drained, fertile soil which does not dry out.

Position: Grow against a wall, to cover a pergola, arch or trellis or to form an effective flowering column by training around a pole or post. Best in sun.

Care: Cut old stems to ground level in late autumn or early spring. Water well during dry periods.

Lonicera × *americana*: Honeysuckle

The principal delight of this vigorous, twining climber must be its delicious fragrance. Given the support of wires it will form a bushy plant bearing a profusion of branched flower-heads in rose-pink, white and creamy-yellow throughout the summer and into autumn.

Height × spread: Climbing to 7m/23ft or more.

Soil: For well drained, fertile soil which does not dry out.

Position: Grow against a wall or use to cover a pergola, arch or trellis. Suitable to screen in season an unsightly building or to disguise an old tree stump. For sun or partial shade.

Care: After flowering, shorten flowered shoots back to new growth. Cut out some old wood and remove unwanted stems.

◐◑ │ ◇ │ ❄❄❄

A vigorous, twining climber valued for its somewhat glaucous stems, blue-green leaves and its heavily scented flowers of purplish-crimson, the insides of which are cream, which appear throughout the summer and into autumn. The perfume is particularly pronounced in the evening.

Height × spread: Climbing to 7m/23ft or more.

Soil: For well drained, fertile soil which does not dry out.

Position: Grow against a wall or use to cover a pergola, arch or trellis. Suitable to screen in season an unsightly building or to disguise an old tree stump. For sun or partial shade.

Care: After flowering, shorten flowered shoots back to new growth. Cut out some old wood and remove unwanted stems.

Lonicera sempervirens: Honeysuckle

An evergreen or semi-evergreen climber of moderate vigour originating in the east and south of the United States of America. Leaves are of deep green, grey-green on the undersides, and are accompanied with clusters of brilliant orange-red flowers, yellow on the insides, in summer. A particularly striking plant which is effective in most garden situations.

Height × spread: Climbing to 4m/13ft or more.

Soil: For well drained, fertile soil which does not dry out.

Position: Best grown against a warm, sheltered wall in full sun or suitable to cover a pergola, arch or trellis.

Care: After flowering, shorten flowered shoots back to new growth. Cut out some old wood and remove unwanted stems.

○ ◊ E or Semi-E LH ❄❄❄

Rather sadly this splendid climber is completely lacking in scent. However, it is well worth growing for its profusion of brilliant, deep yellow flowers, tinged with orange when in bud, which are carried throughout the summer.

Height × spread: Climbing to 5m/16ft or more.

Soil: For well drained, fertile soil which does not dry out.

Position: Not unhappy in sun, *L.* × *tellmanniana* is best given a cool root run and positioned to enjoy partial shade. Grow against a wall, to cover a pergola, arch or trellis or to conceal in season an unsightly building.

Care: After flowering, shorten flowered shoots back to new growth. Cut out some old wood and remove unwanted stems.

◑ ◊ ❋❋❋

Lonicera tragophylla: Honeysuckle

Whilst this climbing honeysuckle remains unscented it is, nevertheless, one of the most splendid of all. Originating in western China, it carries large flowerheads of an intense butter-yellow in summer. Leaves, which are tinged purple, complement the flowers. Red berries follow in autumn.

Height × spread: Climbing to 6m/20ft or more.

Soil: For well drained, fertile soil which does not dry out.

Position: Not unhappy in sun, *L. tragophylla* is best given a cool root run and positioned to enjoy partial or complete shade. Grow against a wall, to cover a pergola, arch or trellis or to conceal in season an unsightly building.

Care: After flowering, shorten flowered shoots back to new growth.

◐ ● │ ◊ │ ✳✳✳

Mandevilla splendens (syn. *Dipladenia*)

A frost tender climber of vigorous growth with twining stems and carrying pink to carmine flowers with a distinctive yellow eye throughout the summer. To flower freely, *Mandevilla* requires a minimum temperature of 15°C/59°F.

Height × spread: Climbing to 3m/10ft or more.

Soil: For well drained, fertile soil which does not dry out.

Position: Except in the warmest of areas, where it may be grown outdoors, this climber is well suited to pot cultivation. Over-winter in a cool conservatory, minimum temperature 7°–10°C/45°–50°F, and place outside for the summer in a sunny, sheltered situation.

Care: During the growing season tie in twining stems to supports. Keep tuberous roots virtually dry in winter when the plant is dormant.

◖ ◊ ❄

Mutisia ilicifolia

A frost hardy, evergreen climber from South America which attaches itself to supports by means of leaf tendrils. Mauve-pink, yellow-centred daisy flowers, in bloom from spring until autumn, are carried over holly-like leaves.

Height × spread: Climbing to 3m/10ft or more.

Soil: For well drained, humus-rich soil which does not dry out.

Position: Best grown against a warm, sheltered wall in full sun where it will require wire supports. In cooler areas grow as a conservatory plant.

Care: Tie in new shoots to supports throughout the growing season. Regularly remove dead leaves which tend to clutter the plant. Ensure that roots are protected from an excess of winter wet.

| ◯ | ◊ | E | ❋❋ |

Oxypetalum caerulea (syn. *Tweedia*)

A most appealing and desirable, frost tender climbing sub-shrub with twining stems carrying grey-green leaves and remarkable sky-blue, starry flowers, fading to lilac-pink, borne in clusters throughout the summer.

Height × spread: Climbing to 1m/3ft or more.

Soil: For well drained, fertile soil which does not dry out.

Position: Except in the warmest of areas, where it may be grown outdoors, this perennial should be treated as a conservatory plant where over winter it should be given a minimum temperature of 5°C/41°F. For sun.

Care: Cut old stems down to ground level in early spring. May be cultivated as an annual from seed or propagated from basal cuttings taken in spring.

Pandorea jasminoides 'Rosea Superba': Bower vine

A frost tender, evergreen climber of vigorous habit with soft green leaves and carrying sprays of trumpet-shaped flowers of pale pink, with deeper crimson throats, in spring and summer and often for a second flush in autumn.

Height × spread: Climbing to 4.5m/15ft or more.

Soil: For well drained, fertile soil which does not dry out.

Position: Except in the warmest of areas where it may be grown outdoors, *Pandorea* should be treated as a conservatory plant where over winter it should be given a minimum temperature of 5°C/41°F. For sun.

Care: Protect over winter in a frost free environment. Cut out an excess of growth.

◯ ◌ E ❋

Parthenocissus henryana

Dark crimson leaves capture the essence of autumn in this self-clinging, vigorous climber from central China. Throughout the spring and summer foliage is bronze-green, the veins standing out in silver-grey. Seen at its most brilliant in autumn when allowed the freedom of a house wall.

Height × spread: Climbing to 10m/33ft or more.

Soil: For well drained, fertile soil which does not dry out.

Position: Best grown against a wall with protection from cold, damaging winds. Avoid positioning in full sun when the marking on the leaves is less pronounced.

Care: Cut back growth in autumn only when it is necessary to keep within bounds.

◐ ● | ◊ | ❋❋❋

A vigorous climber of rapid growth which clings to a host wall by means of small adhesive discs. Divided leaves are of a pleasant, soft green turning to brilliant red in autumn when a mature plant becomes a remarkable sight. Capable of reaching the top of tall buildings as well as festooning itself through trees.

Height × spread: Climbing to 9m/30ft or more.

Soil: For well drained, fertile soil which does not dry out.

Position: Best grown against a wall or planted to climb into and hang from a large tree.

Care: Cut back growth in autumn only when it is necessary to keep within bounds.

Passiflora antioquiensis

This highly desirable, semi-evergreen, frost tender climber supports itself by means of leaf tendrils and produces sumptuous, tubular flowers of rich ruby-red in late summer and autumn. A showy plant for a conservatory or glasshouse where frost is a winter hazard.

Height × spread: Climbing to 6m/20ft or more.

Soil: For well drained, fertile soil which does not dry out.

Position: Except in the warmest of areas where it may be grown outdoors, *P. antioquiensis* should be treated as a conservatory plant where over winter it should be given a minimum temperature of 5°C/41°F. For sun.

Care: Protect over winter in a frost free environment. Cut old stems down to ground level in spring.

| ◯ | ◌ | Semi-E | ❄ |

Passiflora caerulea: Passion flower

Passion flowers are so named as the distinct parts of the flower are said to represent the instruments of Christ's passion. This much admired, frost hardy, semi-evergreen climber is of vigorous habit and attaches itself by means of leaf tendrils. Unusual flowers of blush-white, purple, blue, cream and gold are carried throughout the summer and are followed in hot areas by orange fruits.

Height × spread: Climbing to 6m/20ft or more.

Soil: For well drained, fertile soil which does not dry out.

Position: Best grown against a warm, sheltered wall in full sun. Also suitable to cover a pergola, arch or trellis.

Care: Mulch the base of the plant in winter for added protection. Cut old or dead stems down to ground level in spring.

◐ ◊ Semi-E ❄❄

Passiflora caerulea 'Constance Elliott': Passion flower

Arguably lovelier than the climbing *P. caerulea*, this frost hardy, semi-evergreen form of the passion flower carries beautiful creamy-white flowers over twining stems throughout the summer. Of vigorous habit, it will attain a good height even if cut back in winter.

Height × spread: Climbing to 6m/20ft or more.

Soil: For well drained, fertile soil which does not dry out.

Position: Best grown against a warm, sheltered wall in full sun. Also suitable to cover a pergola, arch or trellis.

Care: Mulch the base of the plant in winter for added protection. Cut old or dead stems down to ground level in spring.

| ☉ | ◊ | Semi-E | ❋❋ |

Polygonum baldschuanicum: Russian vine

A rampant climber which should be planted only in a
situation which calls for virtually uncontrolled growth.
Long, trailing shoots carry heart-shaped, pointed leaves
over which are produced panicles of scented white
flowers in profusion in late summer and autumn.

Height × spread: Climbing to 12m/39ft or more.

Soil: For well drained, fertile soil which does not dry out.

Position: May be used to mask an unsightly building or similar where
vigorous growth will rapidly provide an effective cover in season. For
sun or partial shade.

Care: After flowering cut back shoots to the required spread and take
out any excess of growth. Light pruning throughout the growing season
will not prove harmful.

◐ ◑ │ ◊ │ ❋❋❋

Rhodochiton atrosanguineus

A frost tender climber of exotic appearance originating from Mexico. In colder areas most usually grown as an annual when its red and purple flowers, not dissimilar to those of a fuchsia, are carried throughout the summer. In autumn balloon-like seed capsules appear.

Height × spread: Climbing to 3m/10ft or more.

Soil: For well drained, fertile soil which does not dry out.

Position: Best grown against a warm, sheltered wall in full sun. Afford protection from cold, drying winds.

Care: If grown as an annual, collect seed once the flowering period is over. Otherwise cut spent stems to the ground in spring.

◯ ◇ ✳

Rosa 'Aimée Vibert'

A vigorous, climbing rose with pale pink buds opening to scented, pure white flowers in late summer. Foliage is of a shiny dark green.

Height × spread: Climbing to 5m/16ft or more.

Soil: For any well drained, previously enriched soil.

Position: Suitable to grow against a wall, to cover a pergola, arch, or trellis or to be trained around an appropriate support.

Care: Remove dead, diseased or weak growth in early spring. Cut hard back sideshoots that have flowered. Tie in strong new shoots as they develop. Lightly fork in a handful of bonemeal or similar on the surface of the soil around the shrub in spring. Apply a mulch of well rotted manure.

◯ ◑ | ◇ | ❋❋❋

Rosa 'Albéric Barbier'

A vigorous rambler rose with yellow buds opening to scented, double, creamy-yellow flowers in early to midsummer. Some repeat flowers in late summer. Near-evergreen, shiny foliage of dark green.

Height × spread: Climbing to 6m/20ft or more.

Soil: For any well drained, previously enriched soil.

Position: Suitable to grow into a tree or to cover an arbour. 'Albéric Barbier' is shade tolerant.

Care: After blooming, prune all stems that have flowered to ground level. Train and tie in new shoots as they develop. Lightly fork in a handful of bonemeal or similar on the surface of the soil around the shrub in spring. Apply a mulch of well rotted manure.

○ ◑ | ◊ | Semi-E | ❄❄❄

Rosa 'Albertine'

Although strong growing, this rambler rose is less vigorous than many others and can form a lax shrub. Deeply pink buds open to scented, loosely double copper-pink flowers in midsummer. A deservedly popular rose.

Height × spread: Climbing to 6m/20ft or more.

Soil: For any well drained, previously enriched soil.

Position: Suitable to grow against a wall or to cover a pergola, arch or trellis. May be grown as a specimen in a large shrub border.

Care: After blooming, prune all stems that have flowered to ground level. Train and tie in new shoots as they develop. Lightly fork in a handful of bonemeal or similar on the surface of the soil around the shrub in spring. Apply a mulch of well rotted manure.

◑◐ ◊ ❋❋❋

Rosa 'Alchymist'

Large, double, scented rosette-shaped flowers, opening yellow and deepening to a golden-apricot, are carried on this climbing rose throughout the early summer. May be relied upon to flower over a prolonged period.

Height × spread: Climbing to 4m/13ft or more.

Soil: For any well drained, previously enriched soil.

Position: Suitable to grow against a wall, to cover a pergola, arch, or trellis or to be trained around an appropriate support.

Care: Remove dead, diseased or weak growth in early spring. Cut hard back sideshoots that have flowered. Tie in strong new shoots as they develop. Lightly fork in a handful of bonemeal or similar on the surface of the soil around the shrub in spring. Apply a mulch of well rotted manure.

○ ◑ | ◊ | ❋❋❋

Rosa 'Altissimo'

Where space is possibly restricted, then this climbing rose of compact habit is an ideal choice. Well shaped, single flowers of blood-red, tinged with crimson, and carrying golden stamens, are borne in summer and again at the onset of autumn. May also be grown as a shrub.

Height × spread: Climbing to 2.4m/8ft.

Soil: For any well drained, previously enriched soil.

Position: Suitable to grow against a wall, to cover a pergola, arch, or trellis or to be trained around an appropriate support.

Care: Remove dead, diseased or weak growth in early spring. Cut hard back sideshoots that have flowered. Tie in strong new shoots as they develop. Lightly fork in a handful of bonemeal or similar on the surface of the soil around the shrub in spring. Apply a mulch of well rotted manure.

◐◑ ◊ ❋❋❋

Rosa 'American Pillar'

A summer flowering climbing rose valued for its large clusters of cerise-red flowers with a white eye. Foliage is of a glossy mid-green, turning coppery in the autumn.

Height × spread: Climbing to 3m/10ft or more.

Soil: For any well drained, previously enriched soil.

Position: Suitable to grow against a wall, to cover a pergola, arch, or trellis or to be trained around an appropriate support.

Care: Remove dead, diseased or weak growth in early spring. Cut hard back sideshoots that have flowered. Tie in strong new shoots as they develop. Lightly fork in a handful of bonemeal or similar on the surface of the soil around the shrub in spring. Apply a mulch of well rotted manure.

◐◑ ◊ ✳✳✳

Rosa banksiae 'Lutea'

Almost certainly one of the first roses to flower, this
rambler rose is a mass of double, warm yellow flowers
over fresh green, semi-evergreen foliage in spring. Some
faint scent. On the borderline of hardiness, it must be
afforded a warm wall.

Height × spread: Climbing to 6m/20ft or more.

Soil: For any well drained, previously enriched soil.

Position: Best against a warm, sunny wall out of the reach of cold,
damaging winds.

Care: Little care is required beyond a light prune after flowering has
taken place. Lightly fork in a handful of bonemeal or similar on the
surface of the soil around the shrub in spring. Apply a mulch of well
rotted manure.

| ◯ | ◊ | Semi-E | ❋❋❋ (borderline) |

Rosa 'Blairii Number Two'

Wonderfully scented, this vigorous climbing rose carries globular, double flowers of a rich rose-pink, white at the outer edges, in midsummer. Foliage is of a pleasing dark green.

Height × spread: Climbing to 6m/20ft or more.

Soil: For any well drained, previously enriched soil.

Position: Suitable to grow against a wall, to cover a pergola, arch, or trellis or to be trained around an appropriate support.

Care: Remove dead, diseased or weak growth in early spring. Cut hard back sideshoots that have flowered. Tie in strong new shoots as they develop. Lightly fork in a handful of bonemeal or similar on the surface of the soil around the shrub in spring. Apply a mulch of well rotted manure.

◒◑ | ◊ | ❄❄❄

Rosa 'Bleu Magenta'

A vigorous rambler rose carrying clusters of scented, deep red-purple, small flowers in summer. Both foliage and stems are an attractive shade of light green. Does not repeat flower.

Height × spread: Climbing to 4m/13ft or more.

Soil: For any well drained, previously enriched soil.

Position: Suitable to grow into a tree, to cover an arbour or to train against a wall.

Care: After blooming, prune all stems that have flowered to ground level. Train and tie in new shoots as they develop. Lightly fork in a handful of bonemeal or similar on the surface of the soil around the shrub in spring. Apply a mulch of well rotted manure.

◐◑ | △ | ❄❄❄

Rosa 'Blush Noisette'

Slow to establish, this exceedingly pretty climbing rose carries clusters of semi-double, clove scented, pinky-white flowers continuously throughout the summer and into autumn.

Height × spread: Climbing to 4.5m/15ft or more.

Soil: For any well drained, previously enriched soil.

Position: Suitable to grow against a wall, to cover a pergola, arch, or trellis or to be trained around an appropriate support.

Care: Remove dead, diseased or weak growth in early spring. Cut hard back sideshoots that have flowered. Tie in strong new shoots as they develop. Lightly fork in a handful of bonemeal or similar on the surface of the soil around the shrub in spring. Apply a mulch of well rotted manure.

Rosa 'Bobbie James'

Corymbs of scented, creamy-white, semi-double flowers clothe this vigorous rambler rose in midsummer. An ideal rose with which to cover a large space or to conceal an unsightly building. An abundance of light green foliage.

Height × spread: Climbing to 9m/30ft or more.

Soil: For any well drained, previously enriched soil.

Position: Suitable to grow into a tree, to cover an arbour or to train against a wall.

Care: After blooming, prune all stems that have flowered to ground level. Train and tie in new shoots as they develop. Lightly fork in a handful of bonemeal or similar on the surface of the soil around the shrub in spring. Apply a mulch of well rotted manure.

◐ ◑ │ ◊ │ ❋❋❋

Rosa 'Climbing Cécile Brunner'

A vigorous climbing sport of the well loved bush rose.
Most appealing, beautifully shaped miniature blooms of
blush-pink, slightly scented, are carried in summer over
fresh, disease-resistant foliage.

Height × spread: Climbing to 6m/20ft or more.

Soil: For any well drained, previously enriched soil.

Position: Suitable to grow against a wall, to cover a pergola, arch,
or trellis or to be trained around an appropriate support.

Care: Remove dead, diseased or weak growth in early spring. Cut
hard back sideshoots that have flowered. Tie in strong new shoots as
they develop. Lightly fork in a handful of bonemeal or similar on the
surface of the soil around the shrub in spring. Apply a mulch of well
rotted manure.

◯ ◑ ◊ ❋❋❋

Rosa 'Climbing Iceberg'

A deservedly popular climbing form of the widely grown floribunda rose. Sprays of ice-white flowers are carried in profusion over glossy, dark green foliage continuously throughout the summer.

Height × spread: Climbing to 3m/10ft or more.

Soil: For any well drained, previously enriched soil.

Position: Suitable to grow against a wall, to cover a pergola, arch, or trellis or to be trained around an appropriate support.

Care: Remove dead, diseased or weak growth in early spring. Cut hard back sideshoots that have flowered. Tie in strong new shoots as they develop. Lightly fork in a handful of bonemeal or similar on the surface of the soil around the shrub in spring. Apply a mulch of well rotted manure.

◐ ◑ | ◊ | ✳✳✳

Rosa 'Climbing Lady Hillingdon'

A sport of the bush rose, this climber is best positioned against a warm wall where the loosely double, rich apricot-yellow flowers will bloom throughout the summer and give off their perfume. Good dark green foliage.

Height × spread: Climbing to 5m/16ft or more.

Soil: For any well drained, previously enriched soil.

Position: Suitable to grow against a wall, to cover a pergola, arch, or trellis or to be trained around an appropriate support.

Care: Remove dead, diseased or weak growth in early spring. Cut hard back sideshoots that have flowered. Tie in strong new shoots as they develop. Lightly fork in a handful of bonemeal or similar on the surface of the soil around the shrub in spring. Apply a mulch of well rotted manure.

Rosa 'Climbing Souvenir de la Malmaison'

Another sport of a bush rose, this climber is of vigorous habit and carries scented, flat fronted flowers of peachy-pink in midsummer and again in late summer. Prefers a sunny situation.

Height × spread: Climbing to 5m/16ft or more.

Soil: For any well drained, previously enriched soil.

Position: Suitable to grow against a wall, to cover a pergola, arch, or trellis or to be trained around an appropriate support.

Care: Remove dead, diseased or weak growth in early spring. Cut hard back sideshoots that have flowered. Tie in strong new shoots as they develop. Lightly fork in a handful of bonemeal or similar on the surface of the soil around the shrub in spring. Apply a mulch of well rotted manure.

○ ◊ ✳✳✳

Brilliant scarlet flowers are carried on this climbing form of the hybrid tea rose throughout the summer. Scented flowers are accompanied by good, mid-green foliage.

Height × spread: Climbing to 3m/10ft or more.

Soil: For any well drained, previously enriched soil.

Position: Suitable to grow against a wall, to cover a pergola, arch, or trellis or to be trained around an appropriate support.

Care: Remove dead, diseased or weak growth in early spring. Cut hard back sideshoots that have flowered. Tie in strong new shoots as they develop. Lightly fork in a handful of bonemeal or similar on the surface of the soil around the shrub in spring. Apply a mulch of well rotted manure.

○ ◑ | ◊ | ✽✽✽

Rosa 'Constance Spry'

Generally regarded as one of the loveliest of shrub roses, 'Constance Spry' may easily be trained as a climber when it will delight with a profusion of clear, luminous-pink globe flowers in summer.

Height × spread: Climbing to 2.4m/8ft or more.

Soil: For any well drained, previously enriched soil.

Position: Suitable to grow against a wall, to cover a pergola, arch, or trellis or to be trained around an appropriate support.

Care: Remove dead, diseased or weak growth in early spring. Cut hard back sideshoots that have flowered. Tie in strong new shoots as they develop. Lightly fork in a handful or bonemeal or similar on the surface of the soil around the shrub in spring. Apply a mulch of well rotted manure.

◐◑ △ ❋❋❋

Rosa 'Coral Satin'

This modern climbing rose produces shocking-pink flowers opening from deep pink-red buds throughout the summer. Foliage is of a glossy mid-green. Not an easy colour, but one which is bound to attract attention.

Height × spread: Climbing to 2.4/8ft or more.

Soil: For any well drained, previously enriched soil.

Position: Suitable to grow against a wall, to cover a pergola, arch, or trellis or to be trained around an appropriate support.

Care: Remove dead, diseased or weak growth in early spring. Cut hard back sideshoots that have flowered. Tie in strong new shoots as they develop. Lightly fork in a handful of bonemeal or similar on the surface of the soil around the shrub in spring. Apply a mulch of well rotted manure.

Rosa 'Crimson Shower'

Trusses of crimson-magenta rosettes are freely produced on this vigorous rambler from midsummer through until the onset of autumn. Flowers are slightly scented. Foliage is of a deep, shiny green.

Height × spread: Climbing to 5m/16ft or more.

Soil: For any well drained, previously enriched soil.

Position: Suitable to grow into a tree, to cover an arbour or to train against a wall.

Care: After blooming, prune all stems that have flowered to ground level. Train and tie in new shoots as they develop. Lightly fork in a handful of bonemeal or similar on the surface of the soil around the shrub in spring. Apply a mulch of well rotted manure.

◐ ◑ | ◊ | ❈❈❈

Semi-double, barely scented flowers of scarlet-red with traces of orange are carried on this vigorous, modern climbing rose throughout the summer. Foliage is of a shiny mid-green.

Height × spread: Climbing to 3m/10ft or more.

Soil: For any well drained, previously enriched soil.

Position: Suitable to grow against a wall, to cover a pergola, arch, or trellis or to be trained around an appropriate support. An excellent choice for a shady aspect.

Care: Remove dead, diseased or weak growth in early spring. Cut hard back sideshoots that have flowered. Tie in strong new shoots as they develop. Lightly fork in a handful of bonemeal or similar on the surface of the soil around the shrub in spring. Apply a mulch of well rotted manure.

Rosa 'Félicité et Perpétue'

Virtually evergreen, this rambler rose remains a popular choice. Small, pink-tinted buds open to tightly packed, double, pompon-like, creamy-white flowers which carry a delicate scent throughout midsummer. Totally reliable.

Height × spread: Climbing to 6m/20ft or more.

Soil: For any well drained, previously enriched soil.

Position: Suitable to grow into a tree, to cover an arbour or to train against a wall.

Care: After blooming, prune all stems that have flowered to ground level. Train and tie in new shoots as they develop. Lightly fork in a handful of bonemeal or similar on the surface of the soil around the shrub in spring. Apply a mulch of well rotted manure.

◐ ◑ | ◊ | Semi-E | ✽✽✽

Rosa filipes 'Kiftsgate'

Difficult to resist on account of the profusion of single white, heavily scented flowers which mass over this rambler rose in midsummer to be followed by tiny fruits. However, it is exceedingly rampant and must be afforded an extraordinarily large space.

Height × spread: Climbing to 13m/43ft or more.

Soil: For any well drained, previously enriched soil.

Position: Unsuitable for anywhere other than to grow into a tree or trees capable of withstanding its weight. May be used to conceal an unsightly building.

Care: Once established and gaining maturity little pruning is possible beyond the removal of dead or diseased wood. Young plants should be treated as for all rambler roses.

◐◑ │ ◊ │ ❄❄❄

Rosa 'Francis E. Lester'

A strong growing rambler rose carrying clusters of open cup-shaped flowers, white at the centre and suffused with pink at the edges, in summer. Strongly scented blooms are followed with orange heps in autumn.

Height × spread: Climbing to 4.5m/15ft or more.

Soil: For any well drained, previously enriched soil.

Position: Suitable to grow into a tree, to cover an arbour or to train against a wall.

Care: After blooming, prune all stems that have flowered to ground level. Train and tie in new shoots as they develop. Lightly fork in a handful of bonemeal or similar on the surface of the soil around the shrub in spring. Apply a mulch of well rotted manure.

◐ ◑ | ◊ | ❄❄❄

Rosa 'Gloire de Dijon'

Often to be found in old gardens, this handsome climbing rose produces large, rounded flowerheads of butter-yellow shaded with apricot throughout the summer. Flowers are heavily scented and both stems and foliage are attractive.

Height × spread: Climbing to 4.5m/15ft or more.

Soil: For any well drained, previously enriched soil.

Position: Suitable to grow against a wall, to cover a pergola, arch, or trellis or to be trained around an appropriate support.

Care: Remove dead, diseased or weak growth in early spring. Cut hard back sideshoots that have flowered. Tie in strong new shoots as they develop. Lightly fork in a handful of bonemeal or similar on the surface of the soil around the shrub in spring. Apply a mulch of well rotted manure.

◐◑ ◇ ❄❄❄

Rosa 'Golden Showers'

For almost continuous flowering this climbing rose is difficult to rival. Semi-double blooms of light golden-yellow, fading to cream, possess a pleasing scent and are in evidence from early summer onwards. May be grown as a shrub.

Height × spread: Climbing to 3m/10ft or more.

Soil: For any well drained, previously enriched soil.

Position: Suitable to grow against a wall, to cover a pergola, arch, or trellis or to be trained around an appropriate support. An excellent choice for a shady aspect.

Care: Remove dead, diseased or weak growth in early spring. Cut hard back sideshoots that have flowered. Tie in strong new shoots as they develop. Lightly fork in a handful of bonemeal or similar on the surface of the soil around the shrub in spring. Apply a mulch of well rotted manure.

◐ ● | ◊ | ❋❋❋

Rosa 'Goldfinch'

Clusters of button-like, yellow centred fading to white flowers are produced on this rambler rose, one of few which are yellow, in midsummer. Flowers are scented and the general growth is vigorous.

Height × spread: Climbing to 4m/13ft or more.

Soil: For any well drained, previously enriched soil.

Position: Suitable to grow into a tree, to cover an arbour or to train against a wall.

Care: After blooming, prune all stems that have flowered to ground level. Train and tie in new shoots as they develop. Lightly fork in a handful of bonemeal or similar on the surface of the soil around the shrub in spring. Apply a mulch of well rotted manure.

◐◑ ◊ ✻✻✻

Rosa 'Guinée'

Wonderful, velvet-crimson flowers possessing a heady scent are the principal attraction of this spectacular climbing rose. Best set against a dark background to appreciate fully the richness of the midsummer blooms.

Height × spread: Climbing to 4.5m/15ft or more.

Soil: For any well drained, previously enriched soil.

Position: Suitable to grow against a wall, to cover a pergola, arch, or trellis or to be trained around an appropriate support.

Care: Remove dead, diseased or weak growth in early spring. Cut hard back sideshoots that have flowered. Tie in strong new shoots as they develop. Lightly fork in a handful of bonemeal or similar on the surface of the soil around the shrub in spring. Apply a mulch of well rotted manure.

Rosa 'Handel'

Classified as a modern climber of comparatively recent introduction, 'Handel' is, on account of its moderate growth, an ideal rose for the smaller garden. Flowers, in character close to the modern hybrid tea, are of a creamy-blush and may be relied upon to flower for a prolonged period in summer.

Height × spread: Climbing to 2.4m/8ft.

Soil: For any well drained, previously enriched soil.

Position: Suitable to grow against a wall, to cover a pergola, arch, or trellis or to be trained around an appropriate support.

Care: Remove dead, diseased or weak growth in early spring. Cut hard back sideshoots that have flowered. Tie in strong new shoots as they develop. Lightly fork in a handful of bonemeal or similar on the surface of the soil around the shrub in spring. Apply a mulch of well rotted manure.

◐◑ ⬥ ❄❄❄

Rosa 'Lawrence Johnston'

Generally considered to be one of the finest of all climbing roses, 'Lawrence Johnston' carries large, semi-double, scented, clear yellow flowers in early summer. Of strong growth it has good, mid-green foliage.

Height × spread: Climbing to 6–9m/20–30ft or more.

Soil: For any well drained, previously enriched soil.

Position: Suitable to grow against a wall, to cover a pergola, arch, or trellis or to be trained around an appropriate support.

Care: Remove dead, diseased or weak growth in early spring. Cut hard back sideshoots that have flowered. Tie in strong new shoots as they develop. Lightly fork in a handful of bonemeal or similar on the surface of the soil around the shrub in spring. Apply a mulch of well rotted manure.

◯◐ | ◊ | ✳✳✳

Rosa 'Madame Alfred Carrière'

Of vigorous habit, this climbing rose is valued for its double, heavily scented, largely white blooms which are produced over a long period throughout the summer. Foliage remains free of disease.

Height × spread: Climbing to 6m/20ft or more.

Soil: For any well drained, previously enriched soil.

Position: Suitable to grow against a wall, to cover a pergola, arch, or trellis or to be trained around an appropriate support. An excellent choice for a shady aspect.

Care: Remove dead, diseased or weak growth in early spring. Cut hard back sideshoots that have flowered. Tie in strong new shoots as they develop. Lightly fork in a handful of bonemeal or similar on the surface of the soil around the shrub in spring. Apply a mulch of well rotted manure.

◑ ● | ◊ | ❄❄❄

Rosa 'Mme. Isaac Pereire'

Strictly speaking this Bourbon rose is a shrub but it may also be treated as a small climber. Handsome, deep green foliage sets off heavily scented, double, rose-madder flowers in bloom throughout the summer.

Height × spread: Climbing to 1.5m/5ft or more.

Soil: For any well drained, previously enriched soil.

Position: Suitable to grow against a wall, to cover a pergola, arch, or trellis or to be trained around an appropriate support.

Care: Remove dead, diseased or weak growth in early spring. Cut hard back sideshoots that have flowered. Tie in strong new shoots as they develop. Lightly fork in a handful of bonemeal or similar on the surface of the soil around the shrub in spring. Apply a mulch of well rotted manure.

◐ ◑ | △ | ❄❄❄

Rosa 'Maigold'

A vigorous climbing rose carrying semi-double, apricot-yellow flowers over glossy, disease-free foliage in summer. Some second flowers are produced at the onset of autumn.

Height × spread: Climbing to 3.5m/12ft or more.

Soil: For any well drained, previously enriched soil. This rose is tolerant of poor conditions.

Position: Suitable to grow against a wall, to cover a pergola, arch, or trellis or to be trained around an appropriate support.

Care: Remove dead, diseased or weak growth in early spring. Cut hard back sideshoots that have flowered. Tie in strong new shoots as they develop. Lightly fork in a handful of bonemeal or similar on the surface of the soil around the shrub in spring. Apply a mulch of well rotted manure.

◐ ◑ ◊ ❀❀❀

Rosa 'Meg'

A climbing rose with single flowers of flat formation delicately shaded in tones of blush pink and pale apricot with prominent golden-red stamens. Flowering in both mid and late summer.

Height × spread: Climbing to 3.5m/12ft or more.

Soil: For any well drained, previously enriched soil.

Position: Suitable to grow against a wall, to cover a pergola, arch, or trellis or to be trained around an appropriate support.

Care: Remove dead, diseased or weak growth in early spring. Cut hard back sideshoots that have flowered. Tie in strong new shoots as they develop. Lightly fork in a handful of bonemeal or similar on the surface of the soil around the shrub in spring. Apply a mulch of well rotted manure.

○ ◑ | ◊ | ✿✿✿

Rosa 'Mermaid'

Possibly one of the best repeat flowering climbing roses
producing large, single blooms of pale sulphur-yellow
throughout the summer. Not fully hardy, it should be
afforded a warm wall. Totally free of disease. Slow to
establish in the first instance.

Height × spread: Climbing to 7.5–9m/25–30ft or more.

Soil: For any well drained, previously enriched soil.

Position: Best against a warm wall out of the reach of cold,
damaging winds in full sun.

Care: Do not prune beyond the removal of any old or dead wood. Tie
in strong new shoots as they develop. Lightly fork in a handful of
bonemeal or similar on the surface of the soil around the shrub in
spring. Mulch with well rotted manure.

○ ◊ ❄❄❄ (borderline)

Rosa 'New Dawn'

Of all the relatively modern climbers, 'New Dawn' maintains its popularity. Clusters of scented, silver-pink flowers are produced continuously throughout the summer over deep green, glossy foliage.

Height × spread: Climbing to 5m/16ft or more.

Soil: For any well drained, previously enriched soil.

Position: Suitable to grow against a wall, to cover a pergola, arch, or trellis or to be trained around an appropriate support.

Care: Remove dead, diseased or weak growth in early spring. Cut hard back sideshoots that have flowered. Tie in strong new shoots as they develop. Lightly fork in a handful of bonemeal or similar on the surface of the soil around the shrub in spring. Apply a mulch of well rotted manure.

◐ ◑ │ △ │ ✳✳✳

Rosa 'Parkdirektor Riggers'

Clusters of deep crimson flowers are set against dark green, shiny foliage on this easy and vigorous climbing rose. In flower throughout the summer making it a very garden worthy plant.

Height × spread: Climbing to 3.5m/12ft or more.

Soil: For any well drained, previously enriched soil.

Position: Suitable to grow against a wall, to cover a pergola, arch, or trellis or to be trained around an appropriate support.

Care: Remove dead, diseased or weak growth in early spring. Cut hard back sideshoots that have flowered. Tie in strong new shoots as they develop. Lightly fork in a handful of bonemeal or similar on the surface of the soil around the shrub in spring. Apply a mulch of well rotted manure.

○ ◑ | ◊ | ✱✱✱

A lovely, desirable rambler rose. Long, trailing stems carry elegant sprays of blush-pink rosettes in profusion during the early summer. An excellent choice for both grace and vigour.

Height × spread: Climbing to 9m/30ft or more.

Soil: For any well drained, previously enriched soil.

Position: Suitable to grow into a tree, to cover an arbour or to train against a wall.

Care: After blooming, prune all stems that have flowered to ground level. Train and tie in new shoots as they develop. Lightly fork in a handful of bonemeal or similar on the surface of the soil around the shrub in spring. Apply a mulch of well rotted manure.

◐ | ◌ | ✳✳✳

Rosa 'Paul's Scarlet Climber'

Clusters of brilliant scarlet flowers are carried on this climbing rose in summer with a few repeat blooms later on. In recent years its popularity has declined with the introduction of newer, brighter reds.

Height × spread: Climbing to 3m/10ft or more.

Soil: For any well drained, previously enriched soil.

Position: Suitable to grow against a wall, to cover a pergola, arch, or trellis or to be trained around an appropriate support.

Care: Remove dead, diseased or weak growth in early spring. Cut hard back sideshoots that have flowered. Tie in strong new shoots as they develop. Lightly fork in a handful of bonemeal or similar on the surface of the soil around the shrub in spring. Apply a mulch of well rotted manure.

Rosa 'Phyllis Bide'

The unusual colouring of this hybrid rambler rose is almost certain to command attention. Scented flowers, carried throughout the summer, are in shades of lemon, salmon, pink and red and are set against shiny foliage of mid-green. Of limited growth.

Height × spread: Climbing to 3m/10ft or more.

Soil: For any well drained, previously enriched soil.

Position: Suitable to grow against a wall, to cover a pergola, arch or trellis or to be trained around an appropriate support.

Care: After blooming, prune all stems that have flowered to ground level. Train and tie in new shoots as they develop. Lightly fork in a handful of bonemeal or similar on the surface of the soil around the shrub in spring. Apply a mulch of well rotted manure.

◐◑ ◊ ❄❄❄

Rosa 'Pink Perpétue'

One of the modern climbing roses which may be relied upon to flower freely. Trusses of clear, slightly scented, rose-pink flowers are carried over mid-green foliage throughout the summer. Recommended as a pillar rose.

Height × spread: Climbing to 4.5m/15ft or more.

Soil: For any well drained, previously enriched soil.

Position: Suitable to grow against a wall, to cover a pergola, arch or trellis or to be trained around an appropriate support.

Care: Remove dead, diseased or weak growth in early spring. Cut hard back sideshoots that have flowered. Tie in strong new shoots as they develop. Lightly fork in a handful of bonemeal or similar on the surface of the soil around the shrub in spring. Apply a mulch of well rotted manure.

○ ◑ | ◇ | ❋❋❋

Rosa 'Princesse Marie'

Clusters of pretty, pale pink flowers, deeper towards the centre, are carried on this rambling rose in midsummer. Of strong growth, it is ideal for any situation in which it can be allowed to grow unrestricted. Team it with a clematis of complementary colour for heightened effect.

Height × spread: Climbing to 4.5m/15ft.

Soil: For any well drained, previously enriched soil.

Position: Suitable to grow into a tree, to cover an arbour or to train against a wall.

Care: After blooming, prune all stems that have flowered to ground level. Tie in strong new shoots as they develop. Lightly fork in a handful of bonemeal or similar on the surface of the soil around the shrub in spring. Apply a mulch of well rotted manure.

Rosa 'Rambling Rector'

Clusters of small, scented, semi-double flowers of creamy-white smother this rambler rose in summer to be followed with numerous heps in autumn. May, if required, be grown as a large shrub given ample space.

Height × spread: Climbing to 6m/20ft or more.

Soil: For any well drained, previously enriched soil.

Position: Suitable to grow into a tree, to cover an arbour or to train against a wall.

Care: After blooming, prune all stems that have flowered to ground level. Train and tie in new shoots as they develop. Lightly fork in a handful of bonemeal or similar on the surface of the soil around the shrub in spring. Apply a mulch of well rotted manure.

○ ◑ | ◊ | ❄❄❄

Rosa 'Swan Lake'

This modern climbing rose is well suited to the smaller garden on account of its limited growth. Throughout the summer it carries white hybrid tea flowers flushed with some pink over good, mid-green foliage.

Height × spread: Climbing to 2.4m/8ft or more.

Soil: For any well drained, previously enriched soil.

Position: Suitable to grow against a wall, to cover a pergola, arch, or trellis or to be trained around an appropriate support.

Care: Remove dead, diseased or weak growth in early spring. Cut hard back sideshoots that have flowered. Tie in strong new shoots as they develop. Lightly fork in a handful of bonemeal or similar on the surface of the soil around the shrub in spring. Apply a mulch of well rotted manure.

○ ◑ | ◊ | ❋❋❋

Rosa 'Veilchenblau'

Tightly clustered bunches of deep magenta flowers, often variable and fading to lilac, streaked with white, are carried on this rambler rose in summer. 'Veilchenblau' possesses a rich orange scent, has light green foliage and almost thornless stems.

Height × spread: Climbing to 6m/20ft or more.

Soil: For any well drained, previously enriched soil.

Position: Suitable to grow into a tree, to cover an arbour or to train against a wall.

Care: After blooming, prune all stems that have flowered to ground level. Train and tie in new shoots as they develop. Lightly fork in a handful of bonemeal or similar on the surface of the soil around the shrub in spring. Apply a mulch of well rotted manure.

○ ◑ | △ | ✳✳✳

Rosa 'Wedding Day'

An exceedingly prolific and vigorous rambler rose of exceptional fragrance. Yellow in bud, the flowers open to white with pronounced orange stamens and are carried in summer. Small fruits follow in autumn. An understandably popular rose.

Height × spread: Climbing to 10m/33ft or more.

Soil: For any well drained, previously enriched soil.

Position: Suitable to grow into a tree, to cover an arbour or to train against a wall.

Care: After blooming, prune all stems that have flowered to ground level. Train and tie in new shoots as they develop. Lightly fork in a handful of bonemeal or similar on the surface of the soil around the shrub in spring. Apply a mulch of well rotted manure.

◐ ◑ | ◊ | ✳✳✳

Rosa 'Zéphirine Drouhin'

This thornless Bourbon climbing rose has proved itself to be one of the best of all climbers. Deeply scented flowers of cerise-pink are produced in profusion throughout the summer. May, if required, be grown as a shrub.

Height × spread: Climbing to 5m/16ft or more.

Soil: For any well drained, previously enriched soil.

Position: Suitable to grow against a wall, to cover a pergola, arch, or trellis or to be trained around an appropriate support. An excellent choice for a shady aspect.

Care: Remove dead, diseased or weak growth in early spring. Cut hard back sideshoots that have flowered. Tie in strong new shoots as they develop. Lightly fork in a handful of bonemeal or similar on the surface of the soil around the shrub in spring. Apply a mulch of well rotted manure.

◐ ● | △ | ❋❋❋

Solanum jasminoides 'Album': Potato vine

Given warmth and some protection, this vigorous, semi-evergreen climber will reward with clusters of pure white flowers borne in profusion from midsummer until well into autumn. For sheer loveliness it is almost without equal. Twining stems are at their best when allowed to roam freely over a large, dark leafed shrub.

Height × spread: Climbing to 6m/20ft or more.

Soil: For well drained, fertile soil which does not dry out.

Position: Best grown against a warm, sheltered wall in full sun or placed to scramble over a large host shrub or tree. Keep out of the reach of cold, damaging winds.

Care: New stems should, where necessary, be tied in to supports. Remove any dead or weak growth in spring.

○ ◊ Semi-E ❄❄❄ (borderline)

Trachelospermum jasminoides

A highly desirable, evergreen, scented climber whose leaves are of a lustrous, shiny deep green and which form a pleasing mass on an established plant. Starry white flowers in summer later turn to a shade of cream. Flowers are unlikely to be found on young plants.

Height × spread: Climbing to 6m/20ft or more.

Soil: For well drained, fertile soil which does not dry out.

Position: Suitable against a warm, sheltered wall in full sun out of the reach of cold, drying winds. Ideal when sited where the fragrance may be readily appreciated.

Care: No pruning is required. Cut back outward growing shoots close to the wall in spring to retain the overall shape.

| ◯ | ◊ | E | ✳✳✳ |

Tropaeolum speciosum: Flame flower

A twining climber which is much admired on account of its fresh green foliage and, more particularly, the brilliance of its scarlet flowers which are produced in midsummer. *Tropaeolum* will disappear completely during the winter when it may be necessary to mark its position with a cane. Occasionally the flowers are followed by deep blue berries.

Height × spread: Climbing to 2m/6ft or more.

Soil: For well drained, fertile soil which does not dry out.

Position: Shown at its best when flowers are displayed against a dark background. For this *Taxus baccata* (yew) makes an ideal host. For sun or partial shade.

Care: Dies down completely in winter when old stems should be removed.

◐ ◑ | ◊ | ✳✳✳

Tropaeolum tuberosum

A frost hardy climber of moderate growth which arises
from an underground tuber. Twining stems of fresh green
foliage carry orange and flame trumpet-shaped flowers in
summer. An exceedingly striking climber and one which
is seldom generally seen.

Height × spread: Climbing to 1.5m/5ft or more.

Soil: For well drained, fertile soil which does not dry out.

Position: Shown at its best when flowers are displayed against a
dark background. For this *Taxus baccata* (yew) makes an ideal host.
May be grown to fall over a low wall. For sun or partial shade.

Care: Lift tubers in autumn, cover with silver sand and store in a cool
place. In mild areas tubers may be overwintered in the ground.

◯ ◐ ◌ ❄❄

An attractive and vigorous climber which is demanding of much space. Very large leaves, somewhat downy on the undersides, develop from mid-green to the most magnificent crimson and scarlet in the autumn, a colour which is retained over a long period. Small, black grapes provide added interest.

Height × spread: Climbing to 15m/49ft or more.

Soil: For well drained, fertile soil which does not dry out.

Position: Suitable for growing into a large tree, to cover a sizeable pergola or to trail down and over a large bank. For sun or partial shade.

Care: No regular pruning is required. In restricted spaces, prune back to two buds from the framework after leaf fall.

◐ ○ | ◇ | ❋❋❋

Wisteria 'Caroline'

Amongst the most popular and well known of all climbers, wisteria is admired as much for its gnarled stems as for its racemes of flowers. 'Caroline' carries wonderfully scented, bi-coloured, pale lilac and white flowers in early summer with a secondary, smaller crop towards autumn. All *W. sinensis* forms may be relied upon for fragrance.

Height × spread: Climbing to 30m/100ft or more.

Soil: For well drained, fertile soil which does not dry out. Intolerant of chalk.

Position: Well suited to planting against the wall of a house or to cover a pergola. For sun or partial shade.

Care: Prune long growth back to four or five leaves in summer. In winter shorten back to two buds.

◯◑ ◊ ❋❋❋

A well grown climbing wisteria will almost certainly excite interest. Observed in winter, the gnarled wood of a mature specimen of *W. floribunda* is particularly appealing whilst in early summer the long flower racemes of lilac and white carried over fresh green foliage make for an outstanding display.

Height × spread: Climbing to 9m/30ft or more.

Soil: For well drained, fertile soil which does not dry out. Intolerant of chalk.

Position: Well suited to planting against the wall of a house or to cover a pergola. For sun or partial shade.

Care: Prune long growth back to four or five leaves in summer. In winter shorten back to two buds.

◐ ◑ | ◊ | ❄❄❄

Wisteria floribunda 'Alba'

A spectacular climber, this wisteria produces long racemes of pure white flowers in early summer set against fresh green foliage. A lovely plant which will add both grace and elegance to any garden situation. Look out for a pinkish form, 'Rosea', and other named varieties.

Height × spread: Climbing to 9m/30ft or more.

Soil: For well drained, fertile soil which does not dry out. Intolerant of chalk.

Position: Well suited to planting against the wall of a house or to cover a pergola. For sun or partial shade.

Care: Prune long growth back to four or five leaves in summer. In winter shorten back to two buds.

◯◑ | ◊ | ❋❋❋

3.
WALL PLANTS

Abelia schumannii

An elegant and floriferous, semi-evergreen, frost hardy shrub which carries trumpet-shaped flowers of pinky-mauve and white in summer and again at the onset of autumn. Slightly shiny leaves of mid-green are, with stems, inclined to be downy. Associates well with grey and silver leafed plants. With the exception of *A. triflora*, abelias cannot be considered to be fully hardy.

Height × spread: 1.5 × 1.5m/5 × 5ft

Soil: For well drained, fertile soil which does not dry out.

Position: Best grown against a warm, sheltered wall in full sun out of the reach of cold, damaging winds.

Care: No regular pruning. Thin out old wood after flowering. Remove winter damaged growth in spring.

◯ ◌ Semi-E ❄❄

Abeliophyllum distichum

A slow growing, deciduous shrub closely related to forsythia and bearing small, starry, sweetly scented white flowers in the late winter and early spring. Dark green leaves follow the flowers. A valuable addition to the winter garden which, for no apparent reason, is not widely grown. Generally available from good nurseries.

Height × spread: 1.5 × 1.5m/5 × 5ft

Soil: For well drained, fertile soil which does not dry out.

Position: Best grown against a warm, sheltered wall in full sun out of the reach of cold, damaging winds.

Care: No regular pruning. Thin out old wood after flowering. Remove winter damaged growth in spring.

◯ ◊ ❋❋❋

Abutilon megapotamicum

In warmer areas this attractive, frost hardy shrub remains evergreen. Otherwise it should be considered as semi-evergreen. Valued especially for its arching stems which, in summer, carry an abundance of conspicuous, hanging red and yellow flowers. Well worth growing where conditions are available to suit its requirements.

Height × spread: 2.4 × 2m/8 × 6ft

Soil: For well drained, fertile soil which does not dry out.

Position: Best grown against a warm, sheltered wall in full sun out of the reach of cold, damaging winds.

Care: No regular pruning. Thin out old wood after flowering. Remove winter damaged growth in spring.

◖ ◊ E ❄❄

Abutilon vitifolium var. *album*

A frost hardy, deciduous shrub with pleasing foliage of
mid-green and carrying a wealth of white hollyhock-like
flowers with prominent yellow stamens in early summer.
This is a particularly striking shrub which would support
a late flowering clematis to prolong the period of interest
to a later part of the year.

Height × spread: 5 × 2.4m/16 × 8ft

Soil: For well drained, fertile soil which does not dry out.

Position: Best grown against a warm, sheltered wall in full sun out of
the reach of cold, damaging winds.

Care: No regular pruning. Thin out old wood after flowering. Remove
winter damaged growth in spring.

Acca sellowiana: Pineapple guava

Much of the appeal of this rarely grown, frost hardy, evergreen shrub is its attractive foliage comprising grey-green leaves which are white felted on the undersides. Purple-red flowers with long, crimson stamens appear in midsummer to be followed after a hot summer in a warm climate with edible fruits in autumn.

Height × spread: 2 × 2.4m/6 × 8ft

Soil: For well drained, fertile soil which does not dry out.

Position: Best grown against a warm, sheltered wall in full sun out of the reach of cold, damaging winds.

Care: No regular pruning. Thin out old wood after flowering. Remove winter damaged growth in spring.

◯ ◇ E ❄❄

Azara serrata

Given suitably warm, sheltered conditions then this frost hardy, evergreen shrub should succeed. Pretty, rather wispy flowers of a golden-buttercup yellow appearing in spring are set off by showy leaves of shiny, deep green. Flowers carry a delicious scent which, if they are cut and taken indoors, will fill a room.

Height × spread: 2 × 2m/6 × 6ft

Soil: For well drained, fertile soil which does not dry out.

Position: Best grown against a warm, sheltered wall in full sun out of the reach of cold, damaging winds.

Care: No regular pruning. Thin out old wood after flowering. Remove winter damaged growth in spring.

○ ◊ E ❄❄

Buddleja crispa: Butterfly bush

An elegant and desirable, frost hardy shrub whose arching stems carry attractive, woolly-white, hairy leaves and which bears scented, lilac-pink flowers in midsummer. Given sufficient protection, then of all the buddlejas this is the one to choose. Available from any specialist shrub grower or nursery.

Height × spread: 3 × 3m/10 × 10ft

Soil: For well drained, fertile soil which does not dry out.

Position: Best grown against a warm, sheltered wall in full sun out of the reach of cold, damaging winds.

Care: No regular pruning. Thin out old wood after flowering. Remove winter damaged growth in spring.

The common name for this very desirable shrub derives
from the long, bottlebrush-type flowers of creamy-green
made up of countless apparent spikes. Appearing from
late spring to midsummer, they are set off by evergreen,
narrowly tapering leaves of grey-green. For dark red flower
spikes with dull green leaves, grow *C. rigidus*.

Height × spread: 3 × 3m/10 × 10ft

Soil: For well drained, fertile, neutral to acid soil which does not dry
out.

Position: Best grown against a warm, sheltered wall in full sun out of
the reach of cold, damaging winds.

Care: No regular pruning. Thin out old wood after flowering. Remove
winter damaged growth in spring.

| ◯ | ◌ | E | LH | ❊❊ |

Camellia japonica 'Kimberley'

Traditionally camellias are grown as specimen shrubs or trees but there is no reason why they should not be trained against a wall. 'Kimberley' lends itself for this purpose with evergreen leaves of shiny, dark green and single flowers of bright crimson from the early spring.

Height × spread: 3 × 2m/10 × 6ft

Soil: For well drained, fertile, neutral to acid soil which does not dry out.

Position: Best grown against a warm, sheltered wall in a partially shaded situation out of the reach of cold winds and the early morning sun.

Care: No regular pruning. Thin out old wood after flowering. Remove winter damaged growth in spring.

◐ ◊ E LH ❄❄❄

Camellia japonica 'Nobilissima'

Anemone-form flowers of this handsome shrub are of pure white shaded with yellow from the centre outwards. They are borne in profusion from early spring and are set off by the lustrous, evergreen leaves. All camellias will benefit from an annual top dressing of leaf mould or similar.

Height × spread: 3 x 2m/10 x 6ft

Soil: For well drained, fertile, neutral to acid soil which does not dry out.

Position: Best grown against a warm, sheltered wall in a partially shaded situation out of the reach of cold winds and the early morning sun.

Care: No regular pruning. Thin out old wood after flowering. Remove winter damaged growth in spring.

| ◑ | ◊ | E | LH | ❄❄❄ |

Carpenteria californica

This frost hardy, evergreen shrub will delight with its
slightly glossy, leathery leaves of dark green and its
scented, open cup-shaped white flowers with pronounced
yellow stamens which appear in early and midsummer.
Although it may be grown as a specimen shrub, it is well
suited to wall training.

Height × spread: 2 × 2m/6 × 6 ft

Soil: For well drained, fertile soil which does not dry out.

Position: Best grown against a warm, sheltered wall in full sun out of
the reach of cold, damaging winds.

Care: No regular pruning. Thin out old wood after flowering. Remove
winter damaged growth in spring. Older branches may be taken out
periodically to stimulate new growth.

◖ ◌ E ❋❋

Ceanothus arboreus 'Trewithen Blue': California lilac

All ceanothus lend themselves to training against walls where they can be afforded shelter from strong, damaging winds. 'Trewithen Blue' is a frost hardy, evergreen shrub with rounded, dark green leaves and panicles of scented, mid-blue flowers in late spring and early summer.

Height × spread: 6 × 7.5m/20 × 25ft

Soil: For well drained, fertile soil which does not dry out. Tolerant of lime but becoming chlorotic on shallow chalk.

Position: Best grown against a warm, sheltered wall in full sun out of the reach of cold, damaging winds.

Care: No regular pruning. Thin out old wood after flowering. Remove winter damaged growth in spring.

Ceanothus × *delileanus* **'Gloire de Versailles'**: California lilac

This hardy, deciduous shrub is an ideal subject to be trained against a wall. Arching stems of dark green leaves carry panicles of pale blue flowers over a prolonged period from midsummer into autumn. For an added effect, use it as the host for a large flowered, hybrid clematis of complementary colour.

Height × **spread:** 1.5 × 1.5m/5 × 5ft

Soil: For well drained, fertile soil which does not dry out. Tolerant of lime but becoming chlorotic on shallow chalk.

Position: Best grown against a warm, sheltered wall in full sun out of the reach of cold, damaging winds.

Care: Shorten the previous year's growth back to around 10cm/4in in spring. Cut out unwanted stems.

◯ ◊ ❋❋❋

Ceanothus impressus **'Puget Blue'**: California lilac

A vigorous, frost hardy, evergreen shrub which is well
suited to wall training. Leaves, larger than the species, are
of dark green, heavily veined, and show off the profusion
of deep blue flowers which are carried in spring. For pink
late summer flowers, grow the hardy, deciduous *C. ×
pallidus* 'Marie Simon'.

Height × spread: 3 × 3m/10 × 10ft

Soil: For well drained, fertile soil which does not dry out. Tolerant of
lime but becoming chlorotic on shallow chalk.

Position: Best grown against a warm, sheltered wall in full sun out of
the reach of cold, damaging winds.

Care: No regular pruning. Thin out old wood after flowering. Remove
winter damaged growth in spring.

| ◯ | ◊ | E | ❋❋ |

Cestrum elegans 'Smithii'

An elegant and desirable evergreen shrub which is, sadly, frost tender so may only be grown outside in the most favourable of situations. Spreading branches of mid-green leaves carry crimson to pink, tubular flowers from summer to autumn. These are followed by deep red berries. May be treated as a conservatory plant.

Height × spread: 3 × 3m/10 × 10ft

Soil: For well drained, fertile soil which does not dry out.

Position: Best grown against a warm, sheltered wall in full sun out of the reach of cold, damaging winds. Alternatively grow in a container and overwinter in a frost free environment.

Care: No regular pruning. Thin out old wood after flowering. Remove winter damaged growth in spring.

◯ ◇ E ❄

Chaenomeles speciosa 'Cardinalis': Japonica

It is not unusual to see these popular shrubs trained against a wall where, placed in full sun, they will generously flower and fruit. 'Cardinalis' is one such. Of widely spreading habit it carries single scarlet flowers over emerging leaves of shiny dark green in spring. Edible yellow-green fruits follow in autumn.

Height × **spread:** 2.4 × 5m/8 × 16ft

Soil: For well drained, fertile soil which does not dry out.

Position: Although tolerant of partial shade, at its best when grown against a warm, sheltered wall in full sun.

Care: Wall trained shrubs should have the previous year's growth cut back to two or three buds after flowering.

◐◑ | ◊ | ❋❋❋

Chaenomeles speciosa 'Nivalis': Japonica

White flowers hold a particular appeal and those of this widely spreading shrub are no exception. Appearing as the new season's leaves emerge, the single white flowers of spring stand out in marked contrast to the shiny, dark green of the foliage. In autumn yellow fruits are carried. A spectacular shrub for year round interest.

Height × spread: 2.4 × 5m/8 × 16ft

Soil: For well drained, fertile soil which does not dry out.

Position: Although tolerant of partial shade, at its best when grown against a warm, sheltered wall in full sun.

Care: Wall trained shrubs should have the previous year's growth cut back to two or three buds after flowering.

○ ◑ | ◇ | ❄❄❄

Much favoured on account of the sweetly scented flowers which open in winter, this shrub is well suited to growing against a wall where unripened wood is given some protection from extremes of cold. Waxy, bowl-shaped flowers of soft yellow are carried on bare wood before the emergence of shiny, mid-green leaves.

Height × **spread:** 4 × 3m/13 × 10ft

Soil: For well drained, fertile soil which does not dry out.

Position: Best grown against a warm, sheltered wall in full sun out of the reach of cold, damaging winds.

Care: Immediately after flowering reduce flowering stems by half. Thin out any old and crowded branches.

Choisya 'Aztec Pearl': Mexican orange blossom

Grow this attractive evergreen shrub in front of a wall where it will be protected from extremes of cold and wind damage. Finely cut, tapering leaves of mid-green are massed with star-shaped, white flowers, flushed pink, both in spring and again in late summer and autumn. Easy in cultivation, it is a most worthwhile garden plant.

Height × spread: 2.4 × 2.4m/8 × 8ft

Soil: For well drained, fertile soil which does not dry out.

Position: Best grown against a warm, sheltered wall in full sun out of the reach of cold, damaging winds.

Care: No regular pruning. Thin out old wood after flowering. Remove winter damaged growth in spring.

○ ◊ E ❋❋❋

Choisya ternata: Mexican orange blossom

The somewhat brittle stems of this evergreen shrub are easily damaged by strong winds or heavy falls of snow. Providing it with wall protection will help to counter this. Dark green leaves, broader than those of 'Aztec Pearl', are a foil to strongly scented, starry white flowers in late spring, repeated in late summer and autumn.

Height × spread: 2.4 × 2.4m/8 × 8ft

Soil: For well drained, fertile soil which does not dry out.

Position: Best grown against a warm, sheltered wall in full sun out of the reach of cold, damaging winds.

Care: No regular pruning. Thin out old wood after flowering. Remove winter damaged growth in spring.

❍ ◊ E ❄❄❄

Cotoneaster horizontalis

This is an excellent shrub to place against a wall where its outwardly extending branches may be trained to form an interesting and appealing herring-bone pattern. Shiny dark leaves, reddening in autumn, are accompanied with pinky-white flowers in late spring and red berries towards the close of year.

Height × spread: 1 × 1.5m/3 × 5ft or more.

Soil: For well drained, fertile soil which does not dry out. Tolerant of a wide range of conditions.

Position: Best grown against a warm, sheltered wall in sun or partial shade out of the reach of cold, damaging winds.

Care: No regular pruning. Thin out old wood after flowering. Remove winter damaged growth in spring.

○ ◑ | ◊ | ✳✳✳

Crinodendron hookerianum: Lantern tree

An appealing and unusual frost hardy, evergreen shrub which, given the right growing conditions, will reward with a display of lantern-shaped flowers in shades of scarlet to carmine-pink from late spring to late summer. Leaves are of dark green tapering to a fine point.

Height × spread: 6 × 5m/20 × 16ft

Soil: For well drained, acidic soil which does not dry out and which is regularly enriched with humus. Unsuitable for alkaline soils.

Position: Best grown against a warm, sheltered wall in full sun out of the reach of cold, damaging winds.

Care: No regular pruning. Thin out old wood after flowering. Remove winter damaged growth in spring.

○ ◊ E LH ❄❄

Cytisus battandieri: Pineapple broom

Given the protection of a warm wall, against which it may be trained, then this lovely, frost hardy shrub should withstand a certain amount of cold. Racemes of pineapple scented, yellow flowers of upright habit are carried over silvery-grey leaves throughout the summer. Unlikely to succeed in cold gardens or those which suffer from strong winds.

Height × spread: 5 × 5m/16 × 16ft

Soil: For well drained, acidic soil which does not dry out. Unsuitable for alkaline soils.

Position: Best grown against a warm, sheltered wall in full sun out of the reach of cold, damaging winds.

Care: Immediately after flowering reduce the previous year's growth by half. Avoid cutting into old wood.

Drimys lanceolata

Although strictly speaking it is not necessary to grow this frost hardy, evergreen shrub against a wall, the added protection is likely to cause it to come through most winters unscathed. Shiny, dark green leaves, slightly tapering, set off clusters of small, creamy-white flowers in spring.

Height × spread: 1.5 × 1.5m/5 × 5ft

Soil: For well drained, fertile soil which does not dry out.

Position: Best grown against a warm, sheltered wall in sun or partial shade out of the reach of cold, damaging winds.

Care: No regular pruning. Thin out old wood after flowering. Remove winter damaged growth in spring.

Euonymus fortunei 'Silver Queen': Spindle tree

Mainly grown for its variegated foliage, this evergreen cultivar of the spindle tree may readily be trained against a wall to form an interesting and attractive feature. Although the flowers and autumn fruits are insignificant, the dark green leaves, broadly margined white and later tinged pink, provide a sense of lightness all through the year.

Height × spread: 2.4 × 1.5m/8 × 5ft

Soil: For well drained, fertile soil which does not dry out.

Position: Either position in the mixed shrub border or grow against a wall, where it may be trained, in sun or partial shade.

Care: No regular pruning. Remove any unwanted shoots in the spring. Take out any stems which show signs of reverting.

○ ◑ | ◌ | E | ❋❋❋

Fremontodendron 'California Glory': Flannel bush

The spreading habit of this frost hardy, evergreen shrub makes it well suited to wall training. Furthermore, it will enjoy the protection from cold that a wall provides. Generously flowering, the open, cup-shaped flowers of butter-yellow may be enjoyed on and off from late spring to autumn. May lose leaves in periods of extreme cold.

Height × spread: 6 × 4m/20 × 13ft

Soil: For well drained, fertile soil which does not dry out.

Position: Best grown against a warm, sheltered wall in full sun out of the reach of cold, damaging winds.

Care: No regular pruning. Thin out old wood after flowering. Remove winter damaged growth in spring.

○ ◊ E ✳✳

Hoheria lyallii

In warmer areas this elegant, frost hardy, spreading shrub or tree may be grown as a specimen in the open border. Elsewhere it is advisable to place it in front of a wall, or similar, in order to give it necessary protection. Glaucous leaves are massed with large, scented white flowers with prominent purple anthers throughout the midsummer.

Height × spread: 7 × 7m/23 × 23ft

Soil: For well drained, fertile soil which does not dry out.

Position: Best grown against a warm, sheltered wall in full sun out of the reach of cold, damaging winds.

Care: No regular pruning. Thin out old wood after flowering. Remove winter damaged growth in spring.

◖ ◊ ❄❄

Hydrangea quercifolia: Oak-leafed hydrangea

One of the main attractions of this shrub is the appearance of its leaves of mid-green which are cut like those of an oak, hence the common name, and which turn to a rich shade of grape purple in the autumn. To that may be added long panicles of cream flowers, becoming tinged pink with age, which are produced from midsummer to autumn.

Height × spread: 1.5 × 2m/5 × 6ft

Soil: For humus-rich, moist soil which does not dry out.

Position: May be grown as a specimen in a mixed border or placed before a wall to enjoy protection from damaging winds.

Care: No regular pruning. Thin out old wood after flowering. Remove winter damaged growth in spring.

◐◑ | ◊ | ❄❄❄

Itea ilicifolia

Grow this striking, frost hardy, evergreen shrub trained against a wall to enjoy the attractive holly-like leaves all year and, throughout the summer, the showy, catkin-type flowers of ice-green which are scented. A mature specimen is a remarkable sight when in full flower.

Height × spread: 3 × 3m/10 × 10ft

Soil: For well drained, fertile soil which does not dry out. Note that *I. virginica* requires moist, acidic soil in partial shade.

Position: Best grown against a warm, sheltered wall in full sun out of the reach of cold, damaging winds.

Care: No regular pruning. Thin out old wood after flowering. Remove winter damaged growth in spring.

| ◖ | ◌ | E | ❊❊ |

Jasminum nudiflorum: Winter jasmine

Amongst the best known of all winter flowering shrubs, it is well worth training the whippy stems of this jasmine against a wall not only to give a tidy appearance but to ensure a plenteous supply of clear yellow flowers throughout the winter and early spring. In the main flowers are carried on bare wood before the emergence of new leaves.

Height × spread: 3 × 3m/10 × 10ft

Soil: For well drained, fertile soil which does not dry out.

Position: Unfussy as to situation but may be grown against a wall or fence in sun or partial shade.

Care: No regular pruning. Thin out old wood after flowering and remove any unwanted growth.

◐◑ | ◊ | ❄❄❄

Lavatera maritima: Mallow

An evergreen, shrubby perennial of upright habit which may be placed in front of a wall where the somewhat brittle stems will be afforded protection from strong winds. Grey-green leaves set off blush-pink centred, rose flowers throughout the summer. A welcome change from the popular and widely grown sub-shrub, *L.* 'Barnsley'.

Height × spread: 2 × 1m/6 × 3ft

Soil: For well drained, fertile soil which does not dry out.

Position: Best grown against a warm, sheltered wall in full sun out of the reach of cold, damaging winds.

Care: In autumn, shorten shoots by half to reduce wind damage. Hard prune all stems to near ground level in spring.

○ ◊ E ✳✳

It is unfortunate that this delightful, evergreen shrub is frost tender so must be afforded some warmth all winter. Of arching habit, its aromatic leaves are of mid and dark green and it carries a profusion of cup-shaped, white flowers in late spring and early summer. In colder areas grow as a conservatory plant.

Height × spread: 3 × 3m/10 × 10ft

Soil: For well drained, fertile soil which does not dry out.

Position: Grow outside in warm areas against a warm, sheltered wall in full sun. Protect from frost.

Care: No regular pruning. Thin out old wood after flowering. Remove winter damaged growth in spring.

Magnolia grandiflora 'Exmouth'

Often positioned to grow against the wall of a house where it will, in time, grow to become a large, evergreen tree, this summer flowering magnolia is a most handsome addition to any garden. Large creamy-white, scented flowers are carried over deep green, leathery leaves in mid to late summer. Magnolias are good subjects to act as hosts for moderate climbers.

Height × spread: 10 × 10m/33 × 33ft

Soil: For well drained, fertile soil which does not dry out.

Position: Best grown against a warm, sheltered wall in full sun out of the reach of cold, damaging winds.

Care: No regular pruning is required. Remove any damaged or unwanted branches after flowering.

◖ ◊ E ❋❋❋

Mahonia lomariifolia

Place this frost hardy, evergreen shrub against a wall for added protection from winter cold. An elegant shrub of upright habit, it carries erect racemes of scented, pale yellow flowers from late autumn to early spring. These are followed by blue-purple berries. Altogether vastly superior to many of the other mahonias regularly offered for sale.

Height × spread: 3 × 2m/10 × 6ft

Soil: For well drained, fertile soil which does not dry out.

Position: Best grown against a warm, sheltered wall in full sun out of the reach of cold, damaging winds.

Care: No regular pruning. Thin out old wood after flowering. Remove winter damaged growth in spring.

○ ◌ E ❄❄

Malvastrum lateritum

This delightful little perennial is included here on account of its trailing habit and its preference for a warm, sunny situation. Lightly shaded, terracotta flowers with a distinct brick-red and golden eye are carried throughout the summer. Foliage is of a pleasant light green.

Height × spread: Trailing to 1.2m/4ft or more.

Soil: For well drained, fertile soil which does not dry out.

Position: Best planted in a sheltered, sunny spot, such as in front of a wall, where it may climb into the lower reaches of a neighbouring shrub.

Care: Cut down to ground level in the late autumn or early spring.

◐ ◊ ❄❄❄

Mimulus glutinosus

A sunny, warm spot, such as may be found in front of a wall, is an ideal situation for this bright, frost hardy mimulus. Narrow, light green leaves, carried on sticky stems, set off a succession of trumpet-shaped flowers of golden-orange throughout the summer.

Height × **spread:** 1.2 × 1.2m/4 × 4ft

Soil: Best in moisture retentive, humus-rich soil. Intolerant of dry conditions.

Position: Best grown against a warm, sheltered wall in full sun. Protect in winter from extremes of cold by applying a thick mulch around the base of stems.

Care: No regular pruning. Thin out old wood after flowering. Remove winter damaged growth in spring.

Olearia cheesemanii: Daisy bush

Position this shrub in the shelter of a wall. Dark green, tapering leaves are downy-white on the undersides and are a feature of this particular species. Conspicuous daisy-like flowers are carried in clusters in late spring and early summer. Olearias are handsome shrubs which are well worth including in the garden.

Height × spread: 2.4 × 2.4m/8 × 8ft

Soil: For well drained, fertile soil which does not dry out.

Position: Best grown against a warm, sheltered wall in full sun out of the reach of cold, damaging winds.

Care: Frost damaged growth should be pruned back to new shoots in the spring. Olearias will, if required, respond to hard pruning.

⬭ ⬯ ❄❄❄ (borderline)

Philadelphus 'Belle Etoile': Mock orange

The arching stems of this popular shrub look especially good when placed to front a wall. Its single, cup-shaped, highly scented flowers, pale purple at the centre, will enjoy the warmth during the flowering period of late spring and early summer. Tapering leaves are of mid-green.

Height × spread: 2 × 2.4m/6 × 8ft

Soil: For well drained, fertile soil which does not dry out.

Position: May be grown as a specimen in a mixed border. Well suited to placing in front of a warm wall in sun or partial shade.

Care: Immediately after flowering prune old branches hard back, to ground level if necessary, to promote new growth.

◯◑ ◌ ❄❄❄

Phygelius capensis: Cape figwort

Originating in South Africa, this frost hardy shrub may be grown successfully against a sunny wall where it will delight with its tubular flowers of brilliant red with a yellow throat from midsummer until autumn. In colder areas treat as an herbaceous perennial.

Height × **spread:** 2.4 × 1.2m/8 × 4ft

Soil: For well drained, fertile soil which does not dry out.

Position: Best grown against a warm, sheltered wall in full sun out of the reach of cold, damaging winds.

Care: No regular pruning. Thin out old wood after flowering. Remove winter damaged growth in spring. Alternatively cut down to ground level.

◯ ◌ ❄❄

Always admired, pittosporum require a warm, sheltered spot if they are to flourish. This attractive, evergreen shrub is noted for its grey-green leaves edged with white and black stems. Small, maroon flowers are carried in spring. Much in demand by flower arrangers on account of its excellent foliage.

Height × spread: 2.4 × 2.4m/8 × 8ft

Soil: For well drained, fertile soil which does not dry out.

Position: Best grown against a warm, sheltered wall in full sun out of the reach of cold, damaging winds.

Care: No regular pruning. Thin out old wood after flowering. Remove winter damaged growth in spring.

○ ◯ E ❋❋❋ (borderline)

Plumbago capensis

Often treated as a conservatory plant, plumbago needs the protection of a warm wall if it is to be planted out in warmer areas. Its scrambling habit will require the support of wires. Sprays of sky-blue flowers are produced over a prolonged period from summer through until autumn.

Height × spread: Climbing to 4m/13ft or more.

Soil: For well drained, fertile soil which does not dry out.

Position: Best grown against a warm, sheltered wall in full sun out of the reach of cold, damaging winds.

Care: Keep frost free over winter. Hard prune in spring. Provide support for new growth. Increase by taking cuttings in late summer.

◖ ◊ ❄

Noted both for their vigour and their spines, pyracantha shrubs will readily cover a wall in a relatively short space of time. Here the semi-evergreen 'Mohave' is pictured a mass of berry in autumn, the berries following the small, scented white flowers of early summer. If desired pyracantha may be closely clipped to shape; this may result in fewer berries.

Height × spread: 2.4 × 2.4m/8 × 8ft

Soil: For well drained, fertile soil which does not dry out.

Position: Well suited to training against a wall. Tolerant of both sun and shade.

Care: No regular pruning. Thin out old or damaged wood and cut to desired shape in spring.

○ ◑ ● | ◊ | Semi-E | ❊❊❊

A semi-evergreen shrub which lends itself to training against a wall. Creamy-white flowers in early spring are produced in a mass and are heavily scented. These in turn are followed by yellow berries which, once discovered by the birds, will rapidly disappear. Fewer spines than on other forms. Here wires are used to provide a framework.

Height × spread: 2.4 × 2.4m/8 × 8ft

Soil: For well drained, fertile soil which does not dry out.

Position: Well suited to training against a wall. Tolerant of both sun and shade.

Care: No regular pruning. Thin out old or damaged wood and cut to desired shape in spring.

◖ ◑ ● | ◊ | Semi-E | ✷✷✷

Ribes speciosum: Currant

Shown against a light background, the brilliant red of the fuchsia-like flowers of this spiny shrub make an effective and eye-catching show. The flowers, produced in the early spring, contrast well with the leaves of shiny dark green. Graceful in form and habit, this is a shrub which it is difficult to surpass.

Height × spread: 2.4 × 2.4m/8 × 8ft

Soil: For well drained, fertile soil which does not dry out.

Position: Best grown against a warm, sheltered wall in full sun out of the reach of cold, damaging winds.

Care: Take out old or damaged branches and remove unwanted growth immediately after flowering.

○ ◊ ❋❋❋ (borderline)

Salvia confertiflora

This unusual and striking frost hardy salvia from Brazil is seldom seen and requires the warmth and shelter of a wall to succeed. Above the bold green leaves, brown on the undersides, soar tall flower spikes whose inflorescences contain cinnamon flowers surrounded by orange-red calyces. Red flower stalks possess an unpleasant smell.

Height × spread: 1m × 60cm/3 × 2ft

Soil: For well drained, fertile soil which does not dry out.

Position: Best grown against a warm, sheltered wall in full sun. Protect in cold areas from frost.

Care: In cold areas propagate from cuttings in late summer and overwinter in a frost free glasshouse. Alternatively lift, pot and protect from frost.

⏾ 💧 ❄❄

Schizandra rubrifolia

Vertical wires positioned against a wall are necessary to support this climber with its bold leaves of blue-green and bright red flowers in early summer. Later the flowers are followed with fruits which, in appearance, closely resemble a large redcurrant. Well worth taking time and trouble over as this is a rewarding plant to include in the garden.

Height × spread: Climbing to 2.7m/9ft or more.

Soil: For well drained, fertile, soil which does not dry out.

Position: Unfussy as to situation thriving in both sun and partial shade but requiring support.

Care: No regular pruning. Thin out old wood after flowering. Remove winter damaged growth in spring.

Solanum crispum 'Glasnevin'

Although technically a shrub, the frost hardy, evergreen or semi-evergreen solanum is nearly always treated as a climber and trained against a wall. Rich purple, potato-type flowers throughout the summer typify this vigorous form which looks well in association with a late flowering clematis.

Height × spread: Climbing to 6m/20ft or more.

Soil: For well drained, fertile soil which does not dry out.

Position: Best grown against a warm, sheltered wall in full sun out of the reach of cold, damaging winds.

Care: In spring shorten any weak stems and cut back the previous year's growth to retain shape. Tie in new shoots in summer.

◯ ◊ E or Semi-E ❋❋

Solanum dulcamara 'Variegatum': Woody nightshade

Lacking the vigour of *S. crispum* 'Glasnevin', this variegated form is grown principally for its leaves of light green generously splashed with cream at the margins. These contrast well with the violet-purple potato flowers which are produced in summer and which are followed with scarlet, poisonous berries.

Height × spread: Climbing to 2m/6ft or more.

Soil: For well drained, fertile soil which does not dry out.

Position: Best grown against a warm, sheltered wall in full sun out of the reach of cold, damaging winds.

Care: In spring shorten any weak stems and cut back the previous year's growth to retain shape. Tie in new shoots in summer.

◐◑ ◊ ✳✳✳

Index of Common Names

B

Bindweed. See *Convolvulus athaeoides* 120

Blue dawn flower. See *Ipomoea indica* 129

Bower vine. See *Pandorea jasminoides* 144

Butterfly bush. See *Buddleja crispa* 213

C

Californian lilac. See *Ceanothus* species 218–220

Cape figwort. See *Phygelius capensis* 245

Cathedral bell. See *Cobaea scandens* 119

Chilean bellflower. See *Lapageria* 132

Chilean glory vine. See *Eccremocarpus scaber* 121

Chocolate vine. See *Akebia* 116

Climbing hydrangea. See *Hydrangea anomala petiolaris* 128

Crimson glory vine. See *Vitis cognetiae* 202

Currant. See *Ribes speciosum* 250

D

Daisy bush. See *Olearia cheesemanii* 243

Dutchman's pipe. See *Aristolochia durior* 117

F

Firethorn. See *Pyracantha* species 248–249

Flame flower. See *Tropaeolum speciosum* 200

Flannel bush. See *Fremontodendron* 232

G

Golden hop. See *Humulus lupulus* 127

H

Honeysuckle. See *Lonicera* species 136–140

I

Ivy. See *Hedera* species 122–126

J

Japonica. See *Chaenomeles* species 222–223

Jasmine. See *Jasminum* species 130–131

L

Lantern tree. See *Crinodendron hookerianum* 228

Lemon bottlebrush. See *Callistemon pallidus* 214

M

Mallow. See *Lavatera maritima* 237

Mexican orange blossom. See *Choisya* species 225–226

Mock orange. See *Philadelphus* 244

Morning glory. See *Ipomoea indica* 129

O

Oak-leafed hydrangea. See
  Hydrangea quercifolia 234

P

Passion flower. See *Passiflora*
  species 148–149
Perennial pea. See *Lathyrus*
  species 133–135
Pineapple broom. See *Cytisus*
  battandieri 229
Pineapple guava. See *Acca*
  sellowiana 211
Potato vine. See *Solanum*
  jasminoides 198

R

Rose. See *Rosa* 152–197
Russian vine. See *Polygonum*
  baldschuanicum 150

S

Spindle tree. See *Euonymus*
  fortunei 231

T

Tea tree. See *Leptospermum*
  scoparium 238
Trumpet creeper. See *Campsis* ×
  tagliabuana 118

V

Virginia creeper. See
  Parthenocissus quinquefolia
  146

W

Winter jasmine. See *Jasminum*
  nudiflorum 236
Wintersweet. See *Chimonanthus*
  praecox 224
Woody nightshade. See *Solanum*
  dulcamara 'Variegatum' 254